PORTRAIT OF PENRITH AND THE EAST FELLSIDE

By the same author
Portrait of the Howgills and the Upper Eden Valley
Portrait of Kendal and the Kent Valley

Poems
Voices Round a Star
The Beckwalker
Selected Poems
Westmorland Poems
Simon's Garden
The Dame School at Raisbeck

Portrait of

PENRITH AND THE EAST FELLSIDE

by

Michael Ffinch

Photographs by

H. Martin Gardner

ROBERT HALE · LONDON

First published in Great Britain 1985

Robert Hale Limited
Clerkenwell House
Clerkenwell Green
London EC1R 0HT

British Library Cataloguing in Publication Data

Ffinch, Michael
Portrait of Penrith and the East Fellside.—
(Portrait series)
1. Penrith Region (Cumbria)—Description and travel
I. Title II. Series
914.27'86 DA670.P/

ISBN 0-7090-2375-8

Photoset in North Wales by
Derek Doyle & Associates, Mold, Clwyd.
Printed in Great Britain by
St Edmundsbury Press, Bury St Edmunds, Suffolk.
Bound by Hunter & Foulis Limited.

Contents

Illustrations

Preface

What might be called the Land of Penrith includes what for centuries had been dignified by the title of the Honour of Penrith and lies between two ranges of very high hills: the northern extent of the Lakeland fells, with familiar names like Blencathra and Skiddaw, to the west; and the Pennine Range, with Cross Fell as its highest point, to the east. Here the River Eden, swelled continually by its tributaries, makes an ever-widening valley of rich pastureland.

This landscape dominated by the Eden with its many surprises and obvious beauty has been described often enough, but much less has been written about its history and traditions. The purpose of this book is to place Penrith and the surrounding villages in an historical context.

It might be said without exaggeration that historical perspective, like beauty, is in the eye of the beholder, and it amuses me to recall that when I began to delve into Penrith's past I had been happy to notice on one of my earliest visits that the town had a genuine Salutation Inn. What caught my eye immediately was the inn-sign. Some might have considered it too medieval, others too superstitious, but it was at any rate an accurate inn-sign, for it showed the Angel Gabriel announcing his heavenly message to Mary. Someone in Penrith knows their history, I had thought, and felt encouraged. However, when over a year later and my task was completed I happened to pass the same Salutation Inn and I received a stunning blow, for instead of seeing my angel afire with all the refulgence of Heaven I was confronted by two puritanical looking gentlemen hot-foot from the decks of the Mayflower, and, I suspect, bearing the hot coals of Hell-fire, if not on their backs, at least in their minds. Here was a history lesson indeed. The good landlady informed me that the brewery felt the new sign was more 'meaningful' and suited the town better, but that she personally preferred the old one. Good for her.

I tell the tale only to emphasize the fact that history is alive, and certainly kicking, in Penrith!

I should like to thank all those who have helped me in various ways while I have worked on this book: Lady Caroline Howard for lending me useful information about the Dacre Family; Canon Gordon Scott, Mr Freddie Markham, Mr Lawrence James, Fr Thomas Walsh, Miss Judy Medrington of the Institute of Archaeology, Mr Graeme Soffe, Mrs Christine Strickland of the Local History Section of the Kendal Branch of the Cumbria County library, the Headmaster of Sedbergh School, Mr John Strutt, Mr Christopher Hollett, and lastly my thanks are particularly due to my friend Martin Gardner for once again taking such excellent photographs.

For George and June
with love

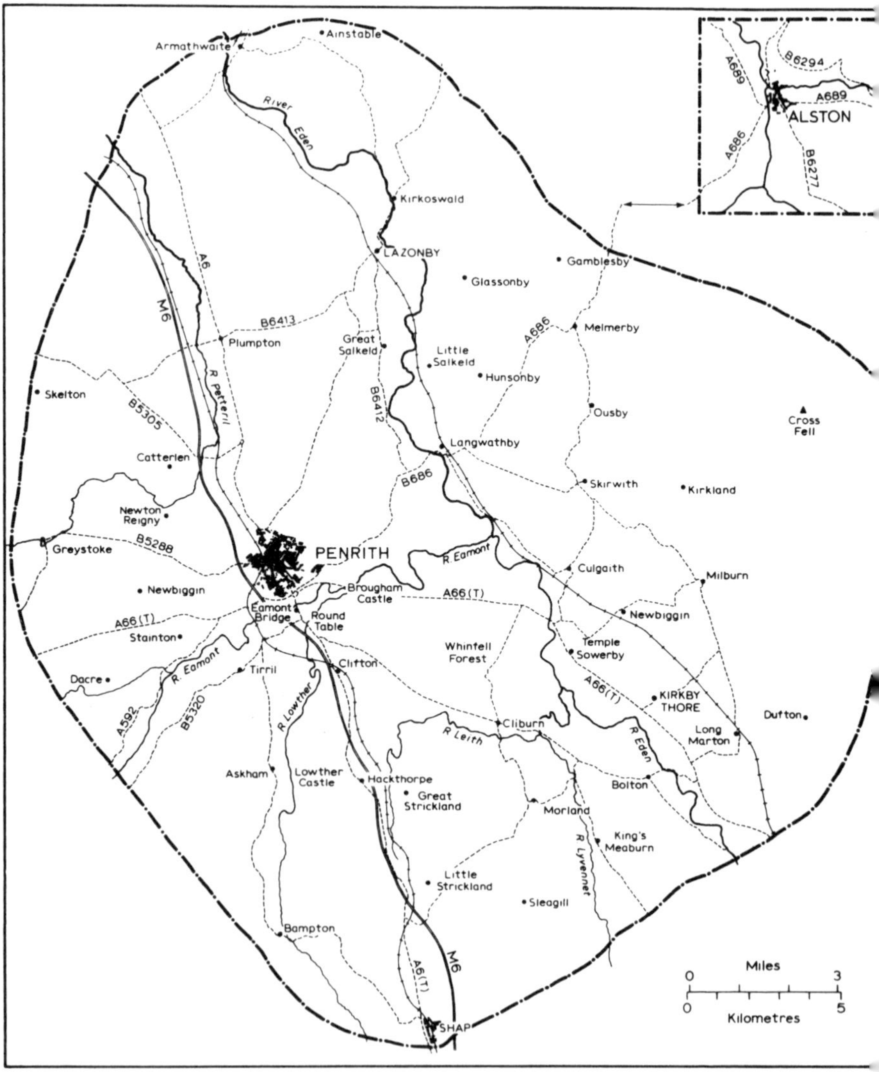
Armathwaite
Ainstable
River Eden
Kirkoswald
LAZONBY
Gamblesby
Glassonby
A6
M6
B6413
Plumpton
Great Salkeld
Little Salkeld
A686
Melmerby
Hunsonby
Skelton
B5305
R. Petteril
B6412
Ousby
Cross Fell
Langwathby
Catterlen
B686
Skirwith
Kirkland
Newton Reigny
B5288
Greystoke
PENRITH
R. Eamont
Culgaith
Milburn
Newbiggin
Brougham Castle
A66(T)
Eamont Bridge
Round Table
Newbiggin
A66(T)
Stainton
Whinfell Forest
Temple Sowerby
R. Eamont
Clifton
Dacre
Tirril
A66(T)
KIRKBY THORE
Dufton
A592
B5320
R. Lowther
Cliburn
R. Leith
R. Eden
Long Marton
Askham
Lowther Castle
Hackthorpe
Great Strickland
Bolton
Morland
King's Meaburn
R. Lyvennet
Little Strickland
Sleagill
Bampton
A6(T)
M6
SHAP
Miles
0
3
0
5
Kilometres
B6294
A689
A689
ALSTON
A686
B6277

1

The Old Red Town

He passed red Penrith's Table Round
For deeds of chivalry renowed
Sir Walter Scott

It was a Tuesday during the summer of 1698 and market day in Penrith when Celia Fiennes, a lady in her early thirties from Wiltshire, riding side-saddle and accompanied by two serving girls, entered the town from the direction of Ullswater. She was struck immediately by the colour of the houses, so much so that she thought the buildings must be of brick, but she soon realized it was the stone which 'in the Quarrys looks very red'.

It is a pity Celia Fiennes did not give a more detailed description of the town, though she did notice several 'Gentleman's houses' and a fine clock on the church tower. She had very much more to say about Lowther, four miles away, as we shall see, but at the time it was important to keep on the move, for she was on what she called her 'Great Journey'. Nevertheless, she had been aroused by what most people notice first about Penrith, especially if they have approached it from the Kendal direction: the complete change in the colour of the rock. While Kendal is limestone, grim and grey, Penrith is sandstone, bright and rosy.

It was the Arabian city of Petra that was once described as the 'rose red city half as old as time', but the line might well be applied to Penrith, and, as it happens, there is more than a similarity of rock-tone between these places for, though situated at opposite ends of the Empire, each was of importance to the Romans. In fact, it was at about the time Petra became part of a Roman province that Penrith was developed as one in a line of forts along the important Second Iter, the road from York to Carlisle. Petra is still known to Europeans by its Latin name, and it would have been a happy coincidence had William Camden been correct in supposing at the end of the sixteenth century that the military station at Old Penrith, situated some five miles north of the present town, had been the Roman Petriana. However, later scholars spoiled the coincidence by identifying the Penrith fort as Voreda, while Petriana turned out to have been at Stanwix, north of Carlisle, on the Roman Wall. Yet there is a further coincidence – as Milton might say, 'happier far' – because both places seem greatly blest by their proximity, in name at least, to that most ancient home of all, Eden.

Had Celia Fiennes chosen to approach Penrith along the Eden Valley, she would have become accustomed to the redness. She would have met it at Appleby, Kirkby Thore and Temple Sowerby, because as soon as the river slips past Kirkby Stephen, it runs along an ever-widening bed of rust-coloured sandstone which geologists have called in many places Penrith Sandstone, a Triassic rock some 200 million years old.

My intention is to give some account of the history and traditions not only of the old red town itself but also of the many villages that surround it. The early stages of the Eden's journey, from its infancy high on the tops of the Mallerstang fells to its sudden turn northward towards Kirkby Stephen, Warcop and Appleby, were described in my book about the Howgills. Now I mean to move down the valley, to linger in what might be termed Middle Eden, if not Middle Earth, where, although not strictly situated by the Eden, Penrith is the centre. I shall use from time to time those ancient words, not forgotten but discouraged, 'Cumberland' and 'Westmorland', for it must be remembered that Penrith was always a border town in two senses. Besides being a town of the Borders in the wider sense, it stood almost exactly on the border between the counties of Cumberland and Westmorland. Much seemed to have come to an end when the two counties were united and joined, with that part of Lancashire north of the Sands to form the greater county of Cumbria in 1974, a change in which Cumberland appeared to have sacrificed the least since the names sounded almost the same, but Westmorland might have been lost altogether had not Appleby, the old county town, pleaded successfully to be allowed to call itself in future Appleby-in-Westmorland, a small consolation but better than nothing.

Unlike Appleby-in-Westmorland, Penrith was never the county town. It has ever played second fiddle to Carlisle, and although Penrith too had its castle, it was never the great fortress of the larger city. The town had no walls, for those once intended were never built, and it is not thought to have been a garrison. Nevertheless, it was not lacking in importance, and it was certainly the centre of that southern part of Cumberland known as the Leath Ward in the great Forest of Inglewood.

The term 'ward' may need some explanation. The four northern counties, Northumberland, Durham, Cumberland and Westmorland, were divided into a number of units known as 'wards', a word of Old English origin giving the sense of guarding or protecting. Such units or districts were usually known in the south and west of England as 'hundreds', while Yorkshire uniquely had its 'thridings', the thirdings, better known as the three ridings. Westmorland was divided into four, the East, West, Kendal and Lonsdale Wards, and Cumberland into five, the Eskdale, Cumberland, Leath, Allerdale-below-Derwent and Allerdale-above-Derwent Wards. Although these divisions may have been recognized before the Normans adopted them, the names did not appear in documents until the reign of Edward I.

What might be called the Penrith Area comprises the northern parts of the East and West Wards of Westmorland, lying south of Penrith, and most of the Leath Ward of Cumberland. In this book I shall describe those parishes in the East Ward situated north of Appleby: Crackenthorpe, Brampton, Dufton, Knock, Long Marton, Kirkby Thore, Milburn, Newbiggin and Temple Sowerby; and from the West Ward those parishes to the north and west of Crosby Ravensworth: King's Meaburn, Sleagill, Newby, Strickland, Morland, Bolton, Cliburn, Brougham, Clifton, Askham, Bampton and Shap. The parishes in the Cumberland Leath Ward are mostly mentioned in some way; these are the parish of Penrith itself, Edenhall, Kirkland, Lazonby, Langwathby, Great Salkeld, Kirkoswald, Castle Sowerby, Ousby, Ainstable, Addingham, Melmerby, Croglin, Renwick, Alston, Dacre, Newton Reigny, Hutton, Skelton, Hesket and Greystoke.

The Chief Ford

The River Eden and its tributaries, particularly the rivers Eamont and Petteril, loom large in the story of Penrith, and although the town does not depend on any river in the way that Kendal, say, once depended on the River Kent, it was the fact that there was an important crossing point on the River Eamont, about a mile south of the town, that gave the place its name. 'Penrith' means 'the chief ford'. The first element of the name, '*pen*', is also found in Penruddock and Torpenhow and is an old British word meaning chief or head in the sense of principal or important. The second element is another old British word, '*riton*', meaning a ford, and this is also seen, though somewhat hidden, in Redmain. The earliest record in which the name of the town appears is a document dated 1167 where the name is written 'Penred', but there are many different spellings, and 'Penret', 'Penneret' and 'Penerth' are among those recorded. The familiar spelling 'Penrith' was first recorded in 1242, while 'Pureth' and 'Peareth appear in records of the fourteenth century. This last is interesting because it is the way many local people still pronounce the name, and 'Peryth Castle' is mentioned in a document dated 1511.

From early times Penrith, the chief ford, was the place where several ways met, and the situation has not changed. Today it is the junction between three major roads: the M6 motorway linking London with Carlisle, the old A6, which passes through the centre of the town, and the A66, which links the east and west coasts of England between Middlesbrough and Workington; but in Roman times also Penrith was an important junction.

It was during the governorship of Petillius Cerialis who commanded the Roman forces in Britain from AD 71 to 74 that the legions advanced westward over the Stainmore Pass for the first time and saw the Eden Valley backed by the Howgills and the Lake District mountains beyond – a sight not much different from that seen today except that at the time the fells would have been topped with small scrubby trees, birches mostly and oaks, and the river valley itself was densely wooded. Cerialis is thought to have established marching camps at three places in the area: at Rey Cross, near Brough, at Crackenthorpe, near Appleby, and at Plumton Head, which is about five miles north of Penrith. His troops must have forded the Eden and, further north, the River Eamont, on that first incursion, but the forts Cerialis set up were not meant to be permanent and it is not thought that he ordered that roads be built.

Cerialis's successor, Frontinus, did not venture this far north, but Agricola who followed campaigned extensively in the north, and it was he who established an efficient road system with permanent forts placed strategically along the various routes.

The main Roman road leading north from York divided at a point just beyond Catterick. One way continued north in the direction of Newcastle, with forts situated at many places, some of which still betray their Roman origin, such as Lanchester, Bunchester and Ebchester. Another way led westward towards the Eden Valley and then continued north-westward towards Carlisle. The forts along this road were positioned at Greta Bridge, Bowes, Brough, Kirkby Thore, Brougham, Old Penrith and Carlisle. At Kirkby Thore another important road, the Maiden Way, branched off north-eastwards towards the rich mining region of Alston, while yet another road linking Ribchester with Carlisle came up the eastern side of the Lune Valley and met the York road at Brougham. Running parallel with the latter was the road from Lancaster to Ambleside, with a fort at Kendal, and from Ambleside the most spectacular Roman road in the region, the High Street, linked Ravenglass with Brougham, crossing over the Kentmere Fells at a point 2,718 feet above sea-level.

In all cases it is likely the Romans followed tracks already in use, and the road over Stainmore in particular was part of the route by which Irish copper was transported to the Continent during the Bronze Age. It is thought the mineral wealth of Britain had brought the Romans across the Channel in the first place, and, as we shall see, the lead mines in the Alston district were probably worked by them.

Inevitably there will be more to say of the Romans when I come to describe the sites of the five military forts in the area, but the peoples who came after the Romans were to have more influence, and here there is a problem. Anyone writing about the early history of Cumberland and Westmorland has a difficulty in being certain about events, since the sources are so very few. When the Roman army was recalled from service in Britain, the native population was left to fend for itself. It is true that in many instances the natives took over the sites of the Roman forts and made them their own; well positioned as they were, the forts continued as strategic positions right down to Norman times. It is not surprising, therefore, that the Norman castles at Brougham, Brough and possibly Appleby are situated on the sites of earlier Roman military stations.

During the four hundred years after the Roman evacuation, the country was infiltrated by various strangers, notably the Teutonic folk, the Saxons, Angles and Jutes, in the fourth and fifth centuries, later the Danes and the Norsemen, and lastly the Normans. It is always important to make the distinction between the British and the English when talking about this early period, when to the modern ear they often mean the same thing. The Celtic tribes, such as the Brigantes and Segantes who inhabited the region from the Clyde Valley in the north to the area of North Wales, were known as 'the Cymry', a Welsh word still very much in use, meaning 'the compatriots'. It is not known exactly at what time the Brythonic tribe the Brigantes, or 'Hillmen', were given the name but it was probably during the last days of the Roman occupation when things were beginning to collapse. However, it is easy to see that this name became the origin of both 'Cumberland' and 'Cumbria'. The Romans are said to have disliked the Brigantes' ferocity and their ability to come swiftly into the attack from their hiding-places in the fells, and just as swiftly to return and evade capture in the fastnesses by the lakes.

Whether early historians such as Nennius and Gildas are to be relied upon at all is doubtful, but it is perhaps worth noting that Nennius mentions that King Arthur fought twelve battles in the north which resulted in the northern 'Cymri' being freed from the English invaders. Gildas, the son of a princeling of the Cumbrian region who died in 570, also mentions the battles, while Geoffrey of Monmouth, whose evidence is generally considered unreliable, mentions that Arthur fought a fierce battle near Penrith. Certainly the name of that mighty hero is associated with several places in the area, Arthur's Round Table, at Eamont Bridge, south of Penrith, and Arthuret, north of Carlisle, being but two of them.

Whether these Arthurian stories are true or not, and whether he held back the tide of the English invasion for the Cumbrians for a time, must remain speculation, but one certain thing is that the area around Penrith became associated with the English in a particular way, as we shall now see.

Inglewood Forest

The land of the Cumberland Leath Ward was part of a wide tract of forest which extended southwards from Carlisle to Penrith. It was named Englewood after the Angles, the Teutonic people who began to settle in the region some time during the seventh century. Whether the Angles first entered the Eden Valley from the north following the line of the River Irthing or, like the Romans, came over Stainmore, is not known, but when St Cuthbert came to Carlisle in AD 685, he found an Anglian abbey already established and many Anglian inhabitants. Certainly the Eden Valley became associated with them in a special way, so that the name 'Engla wudu' is mentioned frequently in the cartulary or register of Holme Cultram Abbey after 1150 and considered 'a goodly great forest, full of woods, red deer and fallow, wild swine, and all manner of wild beasts' by the Normans.

The Latin word '*foresta*' meant any wide area of waste ground reserved for hunting but which was not necessarily wooded. Inglewood, however, was described early on as 'full of woods' and particularly well stocked with deer, so much so that Edward I is said to have killed some four hundred bucks and hinds in one day's hunting.

Like the other forests in the realm, Inglewood was Crown property, protected by stringent laws, and very heavy penalties were imposed on poachers. It was administered by men of different ranks who held office of the Crown under the Justice of the Forest. The Justice of the Forest was not interested in Inglewood alone but had overall control of all forests north of the River Trent. Beside the King, only he had the authority to release a prisoner on bail for stealing or killing deer. The office was an important one and was held by persons high in the King's favour. Seldom was the Justice of the Forest a local, unlike his immediate subordinate the Warden of the Forest. Inglewood had its own warden, an office held by a member of one of the important local families, and names such as Morvill and Dacre are found among the list of early Wardens of the Forest.

After the Warden came the foresters, many of whom held hereditary office and were known as foresters in fee. The forester was a gamekeeper who was under oath to the Crown to preserve the game in his allotted area. It would seem from early records that a mounted forester was of a higher rank than one who went about on foot. These records make fascinating reading and give a vivid idea of how meticulously Forest Law was enforced. In 1285, for instance, two men were caught in the act of skinning the fawn of a hind that had died of hunger. Presumably the fawn would have died anyway, but the offenders were arrested by the forester and sent to Carlisle gaol. During the same year one Stephen Howard, and two others, unknown, killed a stag and two hinds in the land of Plumpton, on Wednesday next before the feast of St Barnabas the Apostle. In this case the forester had tracked the offenders down, and the carcases of the beasts were found at Stephen Howard's house. It was an offence to carry bows and arrows in the forest and illegal to have a dog without a warrant. In the reign of Henry III a greyhound belonging to a Carlisle man was used to take three deer by a group of men travelling back from Kirkoswald to Greystoke.

It seems men from every class of society were prone to poaching, and the parson of Edenhall was among those who took a doe in the town of Edenhall on Wednesday before All Saints Day, 1278 and 'two harts above Brounthwaite with greyhounds on Friday after the Purification of the same year, and were received into the house of the parson.' On both occasions the priest had been in the company of Adam Turpe of Edenhall, a noted deer-stealer.

Other important officers in the forest were the verderers, whose duty it was to attend the county courts and see that justice was exercised fairly. Inglewood, like every other forest, would have had four verderers, who were usually chosen from among the knights or local rich landowners. Then there were the regarders, twelve specially chosen knights who were responsible for making a survey of the forest every three years and for reporting any changes in the nature of the area, tree-clearing, planting and the number of swarms of bees known in the forest. Of particular importance were the falcons and hawks nesting in the forest, and many families living in the area today have ancestors who are involved in this important service, for, as I have said, the various offices were often hereditary. For example, members of the de Raughton family were regarders holding land by service of 'keeping the eyries of hawks in the forest of Inglewood' for several generations.

During the reign of Henry III Thomas de Multon claimed the privileges of his ancestors as hereditary forester. The inquisition was heard at Carlisle and makes such interesting reading that I will quote much of it. It would be well perhaps to keep in mind that a 'bailiwick' is really 'bailiffwick' and means the district under the jurisdiction of a bailiff.

Presiding over the proceedings were the Sheriff of Cumberland, the Sheriff of Lancashire and William de Dacre; the verderers and foresters were also present. The purpose of the hearing, as the preamble states, was to decide 'what privileges Thomas de Multon and his predecessors in the office of Forester in Fee of that forest made use of during their terms of office'.

The verderers and foresters agreed that Thomas de Multon was

Forester in Fee of the whole of the King's forest of Inglewood, and

> should pay for his bailiwick ten marks of silver. He is entitled to payment for all escaped animals except swine; he is entitled to payment of escaped swine taken at any period of the year in Plumpton Hay; and to payment for escaped swine in the forest during the close season, that is, a fortnight before and a fortnight after the feast of St John the Baptist, that is 24th June.
>
> He ought to have all dead wood throughout the forest, standing or fallen; dry wood, and all timber not producing fruit; the stump, loppings, and bark of timber, and the following wood: alder, birch, willow, and all windfallen trees, branches, and all the remainder of oaks granted by the King's mandate, except in Plumpton Hay, because he will receive nothing there.

If anyone was caught in the act of felling an oak unlawfully, Thomas de Multon was 'to attack his person according to the forest law, in order that he may come before the Justices of the Forest, and the King will have the attachment and amercement but Thomas the felled oak'.

Throughout the record of the inquisition de Multon is referred to by his Christian name; thus, 'Thomas has the right to hunt in the forest the hare, the fox, the wild cat, the wolf, the badger, the otter, the martin and the squirrel, and all other woodland beasts except the hart and hind, buck and doe, the roe, the wild boar and wild sow, and hawks which were the King's.' The hawks here referred to were kestrels, but Thomas was entitled to falcons, sparrowhawks and muskets, which were a species of sparrowhawk.

De Multon's many perks included 'all honey with its wax throughout the whole of the King's demesne wood', pannage of swine and 'the right of fishing throughout the whole of the King's forest in all waters and woods'.

It is interesting that even the Sheriff and his deputies were not allowed to carry bows and arrows unless under the supervision of the foresters. The foresters themselves were selected by Thomas, who could choose whomever he wished and remove them at will. The long list of privileges ends with a special one: 'Thomas and his predecessors have been accustomed to make charcoal of the loppings and other timber which belong to him by reason of his bailiwick, wherever they wished in the said forest. Also, he is entitled to free right of way for carrying all this wherever he wishes in the forest.'

Inglewood Forest was originally bounded on the eastern side by the River Eden and extended northwards to a point where the Eden takes the waters of the River Irthing. There the boundary followed the Eden's westerly course and included Carlisle. Then it shared a boundary with the Burgh barony, which was roughly the line of the main road from Carlisle to Wigton, the A595, till where that road crosses the River Wampool the forest boundary ran eastward towards Dalston, then turned due south along the line of the upper reaches of the Wampool, known at one time as Shawk Beck. At a point near Caldbeck it followed a south-easterly course towards Penrith at Eamont Bridge.

This meant that the barony of Greystoke was outside the confines of the forest, as was all land east of the Eden, besides the two Westmorland wards. However, Henry II extended the area of the forest on all sides, which meant that some twenty miles on the east bank of the Eden were included, but this extension was to be short lived since Henry III is thought to have reduced the forest area to its original size.

Inglewood never achieved the fame of Sherwood Forest, and the reputation of Adam Bell, Clym of the Clough and William of Cloudesly, well-known outlaws skilled in archery, hardly match up to that of Robin Hood, but Shakespeare referred to Adam Bell in the first scene of *Much Ado about Nothing*, and his name is mentioned several times in literature in connection with archery. There is an early ballad that relates some of the deeds of these famous northern bowmen, the oldest copy of which is in the British Museum. The poem contains several references to the 'English-wood':

Merry it was in the green forest
   Among the leaves green,
Where that men hunt east and west
   With bows and arrows keen;

To raise the deer out of their den;
   Such sights hath oft been seen,

And by three yeomen of the north countrie,
By them it is I mean.

The one of them hight Adam Bell,
The other Clym of the Clough,
The third was William of Cloudesly,
An archer good enough.

They were outlawed for venison,
These yeomen everychone,
They swore them brethren upon a day,
To English-wood for to gone.

The Honour of Penrith

Situated within the confines of Inglewood Forest as they were, the inhabitants of Penrith had restricted rights to cut timber for building. In 1226 a mandate to Thomas de Multon gave the people of Penrith, Salkeld and Langwathby permission to take wood as 'they were accustomed to during the reign of King John'. The inclusion of Langwathby here is of interest because it would seem from other records that it was outside the forest. However, there was never any doubt about Penrith, and it is time now to consider it in more detail.

It is difficult to say with any degree of certainty to what extent the Penrith area was inhabited before Roman times, because the people of the early Bronze Age – that is, folk who lived from about 1900 to 1500 BC – have left few traces of themselves, but it is reasonable to assume the locality would have been in some way occupied, probably by small farming communities who moved about with their flocks from clearing to clearing. The earliest monument in the area is the megalithic circle situated at Little Salkeld known as Long Meg and her Daughters. This assembly of some sixty-eight stones, of which Long Meg, presumably short for 'megalith', is by far the largest, standing about eighteen feet high, is thought to date to some four hundred years before the Roman occupation, but there are other ancient sites of interest near Penrith itself: Maybrough and King Arthur's Round Table, at Eamont Bridge. Archaeological evidence suggests that Eamont Bridge originated during the Bronze Age but developed later, during Romano-British times. Such exceptional sites are rare, as are examples in the area of what are known as 'hut-villages', settlements of pastoral communities who practised a sort of garden-agriculture. These settlements, usually set on high ground for protection, with a wide field of vision, were particularly common in parts of Westmorland, and we shall meet examples such as Castle Hill, in Dufton, and Skirsgill, in Askam parish. In Cumberland such sites were fewer and, as far as I know, there has never been any suggestion that there was a settlement on the most obvious of places, Beacon Hill, above the modern town.

2

Of Castles and Kings

The Cat, the Rat and Lovell our dog
Rule all England under a hog.
William Collingbourne, 1484

The long-disputed border between England and Scotland was finally agreed by formal treaty during the reign of King John in 1237, but that did not mean there would be lasting peace between the two countries, far from it. It did mean that the boundary following the lines of river, beck or burn was determined. Before that time the border regions had been a kind of no-man's-land. What is certain is that the northern English had far more in common with their neighbours the Scots than with their fellow-countrymen in the south, for, as far as London was concerned, Carlisle was 'a far countree', and the border as such would mean more to the administrators than to the folk who lived in the region. Until 1237 the situation had been somewhat different, with Cumbria becoming English or Scottish by turn.

The influence of the Scots for good and ill on the history of Penrith has been considerable. Situated so close to the 'border', Penrith with the rest of Cumberland was until the reign of Edward I as often as not ruled by the Scots, though it seems the Scottish kings considered the king of England to be their overlord. In the year 939, for instance, we find that King Edmund granted Cumbria to Malcolm I of Scotland 'on condition that the heir apparent to the Scottish throne should hold the district and do homage to the Kings of England, as vassal perpetually for the same'. Later, at the time of the Norman invasion, Malcolm III sided with the English nobles, but he was very soon doing homage to William I at Abernethy. As far as the kings of England were concerned, provided the Scottish kings were vassals, it was very much easier to let them have the responsibility of keeping order in such a remote, uncharted region, a region that would be excluded from the survey the Normans were to carry out known to history as Domesday Book.

The situation was to change slightly when William Rufus marched north to capture Carlisle in 1092. From that time Carlisle was to be an English garrison, and the King granted the city and much of the land to the south of it to Ranulph de Briquessart, more commonly known by the nickname 'le Mesquin', 'the scoundrel' or 'wretch', though this is often written 'de meschines' and appears in several other forms. Ranulph's task was to carry out the King's orders to construct a line of fortifications along the Eden Valley; his land, which comprised much of Cumberland and the East and West ward of Westmorland, did not include Alston at the time. Alston would not become part of Cumberland until Henry II reorganized the district in 1177.

It is known that William Rufus settled 'very many peasants with their wives and livestock' into the region from the south. Like the ill-omened 'Plantation of Ulster', this was to ensure loyalty and establish southern English customs in the north. This policy of William's is recorded in the Anglo-Saxon Chronicle, as is the King's command to fortify the Eden Valley.

However, the land about Carlisle almost inevitably became the subject of constant quarrelling as time went on. In 1172 the Scottish king, William the Lion, led a mixed army of Scots and Flemish mercenaries into England. He timed the invasion carefully to coincide with a rebellion led by two sons of Henry II against their father. Although he found Carlisle too well fortified to capture, he laid waste several of the castles built by William Rufus, completely destroying Brough and Appleby castles. Although William was successful thus far, the campaign as a whole went very much against him: he was forced to accept Henry as his overlord and was made to forfeit several strategic castles, including Edinburgh and Sterling, under the terms of a treaty signed in 1174.

The later treaty, of 1237, already mentioned, was not kept, so much so that the Papal Legate, Cardinal Otho, was called upon five years later to negotiate a compromise. The Scots agreed to relinquish their claim in return for two hundred librates of land, a librate being a piece of land that brought in an income of £1 a year. This land was to be made up from manors where there was no castle. Many familiar names were mentioned, and the fact that Penrith appears among them is proof that there was no castle there at the time. Penrith would remain in the hands of the Scots, who held it of the King of England by fealty and homage 'on payment of one soar hawk annually to be delivered at the castle of Carlisle', an English stronghold. This situation was to last until 1295, in the reign of Edward I.

At that time a serious quarrel arose between the two countries when Edward seized from the King of Scotland the manors of Penrith, Sowerby, Langwathby, Great Salkeld, Carleton and Scotby; these were never returned, though two years later the Scots made an attempt to take them back again. As a chronicler of the events put it: 'At this time the praise of God was unheard in any church or monastery throughout the whole country, for the monks, canons, regulars, and other priests, who were ministers of the Lord, fled with the whole people from the face of the enemy. The Scots roved over the country from the feast of St Luke to St Martin's day, inflicting upon all the horrors of unrestrained rapine and bloodshed.' But Penrith was English at last, remaining Crown land until Richard II granted all the above-mentioned manors to Ralph Neville, Lord of Raby, who was created the first Earl of Westmorland. It might be said that by this Westmorland claimed Penrith for its own, something which, psychologically, it has done ever since.

Penrith Castle

Anyone arriving at Penrith by train will quickly notice the ruins of the castle, situated directly opposite the entrance to the station. In fact, when the railway came to Penrith in 1845, the station and the road leading to it absorbed much of the castle site and the necessary filling-in of much of the moat which is today visible only on the south-east and north-east sides. This was almost certainly a dry moat, for the small spring which at one time bubbled up from its bottom would not have been sufficient to fill the moat altogether. In earlier times the marshy ground at the southern end of the castle site would have given added defence, and it was that area which later was to form the goods station.

As castle ruins go, it must be admitted that Penrith is a little dull and, apart from the south-east face, there is precious little to see. What is seen from the Ullswater Road as one enters the town is misleading, and anyone wishing to see what Penrith Castle has to offer should take some time to walk round the ruins. But there is nothing like as much to see here as at Brougham, fortunate in having an able restorer in Lady Anne Clifford. Penrith was never so blessed, and by the beginning of the sixteenth century it was already in a dilapidated state; when a survey was carried out in 1565, most of the wood-work was reported as being rotten. However, I do not wish to suggest that the castle is not important historically, and although it is not known precisely when the castle was built, what is known is of some interest.

Penrith Castle would seem to owe its existence to William Strickland, who owned considerable land in Penrith parish and later became Bishop of Carlisle. He was granted a licence to crenellate a building in 1397. This is thought to have been the tower, originally known as the Bishop's Tower, which stood on the west corner of the building. In 1399 Strickland was granted a further licence to construct a curtain-wall and join this onto the tower.

As Bishop Strickland was the first benefactor of the town, perhaps we should know a little more about him. He was born in about 1340, a member of a cadet branch of the well-known family that originated at Great Strickland but had settled at Sizergh Castle, near Kendal, when Sir William Strickland had married Elizabeth Deincourt in 1239. The Bishop was not one of the Sizergh Stricklands, and little is known of his early life until

1366, when he is mentioned as being an ecclesiastical lawyer. At this time he was not ordained and he was certainly at the time married to Isabel, the daughter of Thomas and Margaret Warcop; by her he had a daughter, named Margaret after her grandmother. Between 1368 and 1369 Strickland was rector first of Stapleton and then of Ousby. It was about this time that he was ordained an acolyte, one of the steps towards the priesthood but an office that did not require a vow of celibacy. Possibly Isabel Strickland died soon after this, and it has been suggested that her husband, to assuage his grief, decided to move to Oxford for a course of study which lasted until 1370, when he was nominated to represent Bishop Appleby of Carlisle in Parliament. In the latter part of 1381 he was ordained deacon and then priest and became the incumbent of the parish of Rothbury, in Northumberland. Then, in the December of 1388, he was given Horncastle. Seven years later, on the death of Bishop Appleby, the dean and chapter elected Strickland as his successor, an appointment which was not sanctioned by the Papacy at the time. However, Strickland did become Bishop of Carlisle in 1400, and the following year he was one of the commissioners appointed to draw up a peace treaty with the Scots. The Bishop was also active in building and restoring his official residences, Bewley first, then Rose Castle, here he ordered the tower to be built that still bears his name. In 1410 he turned his attention to the cathedral and was responsible for building the tower 'from the middle to the top, placing in four bells'.

Bishop Strickland died at Rose Castle on 30 August 1419 and was interred in his own cathedral.

Besides seeing to the town's defences, Bishop Strickland was at pains to improve the water supply. As the antiquarian Dr Burn puts it, 'He was at the expense of draining a watercourse from the River Petterel through this town'. Here the word 'draining' is important, for there was a beck of some kind running through the area which efficient drainage was able to make into a much faster flowing stream. This was the Thaka Beck, and the name itself gives a clue as to its existence before Bishop Strickland's drainage scheme because it is Old Norse. '*Thaka*', meaning thatch, is found in several place-names, denoting a region where reeds for thatching could be gathered. It is to be seen in Thackmire and Thakthwaite, but also in many field-names. What the Bishop ordered was the clearing away of the reeds in order to make a channel for the stream so that the River Petterel was linked with the River Eamont. Part of Thaka Beck which now flows largely underground may still be seen near the Tourist Information Centre in Middlegate.

Personally I find the Bishop's drainage operations more interesting than his defences, but I must now turn to the castle. In my research I have come upon so many conflicting views as to the castle's origin that it would seem as well to say what is known. Whatever form Bishop Strickland's strengthening and crenellation took in 1397, it was not at the time considered to be a castle, for, when Richard II granted Ralph Nevill the manor and town of Penrith in the following year, there was no mention of it. No, it was the next stage of Bishop Strickland's work that saw the beginnings of the castle, when the King, 'by special grace to our beloved William Strickland', allowed him 'to build a curtain wall of stone and lime and join it to the said house'.

As we have seen, the Bishop died in 1419, and it was almost certainly the Neville family that developed the castle after his death. In 1420 Henry V appointed Richard Neville Warden of the West March, by which appointment he became one of the most influential men in the north, and not only in a military sense, although he had shown an ability to command. He was also at this time Justice of the Peace for Westmorland, Cumberland and Durham.

Richard Neville was the son of Ralph Neville, first Earl of Westmorland, by his wife Joan Beaufort, John of Gaunt's daughter by his third wife, Catherine Swynford. Through his marriage to Alice, the daughter and heir of Thomas, Earl of Salisbury, Richard inherited the Salisbury title. For supporting his brother-in-law, Richard, Duke of York, he was executed after the battle of Wakefield in 1460. His wife, Alice, had borne him ten children, of whom the eldest son, also called Richard, became the renowned Warwick 'the Kingmaker', which is how Penrith proudly claims Warwick as a one-time owner of its castle. However, it was not a simple matter of a son inheriting his father's property, for at his death all Salisbury's estate became forfeit and for a short while Penrith Castle was granted to John, Lord Clifford, but he was killed at the battle of Ferrybridge in the following year and 'being attainted, his estates fell to the Crown, and the castle and manor of Penrith were regranted to the Nevilles in the person of Richard, Earl of Warwick'. As Warwick held Penrith for ten years, and at his death it immediately became the property of his son-in-law, Richard, Duke of Gloucester, who is Penrith's proudest boast, I will dwell for a time on their characters.

Born in 1428, Warwick gained the name 'Kingmaker' because of the leading part he played in deposing Henry VI, crowning Edward IV and then turning against Edward and, with the help of Edward's younger brother George, Duke of Clarence, rebelling against his protégé and restoring Henry to the throne in 1470. Edward retaliated and was successful in regaining his kingdom, defeating Warwick at the battle of Barnet, where the Kingmaker was killed.

Warwick's wife, Anne, bore him two children, both girls, Isabel and Anne. Isabel married George, Duke of Clarence, and Anne, the year after her father's death, married Richard, Duke of Gloucester, who as a young man of eighteen had led the right wing of the King's troops at Barnet and had been largely instrumental in bringing about Warwick's defeat. How could Anne marry such a man? As we shall now see, she had known him all her life.

In 1471 Richard, Duke of Gloucester and 'Guardian of the West March toward Scotland', was granted the lordship and castle of Penrith, and it was he who caused another tower to be erected, a porter's lodge together with some attached buildings, and generally transformed the fortified dwelling into a royal 'castle'. Thus it is written, and whereas it seems unlikely that Warwick spent much time at Penrith, there is reason to think Richard knew the town fairly well. There is a deed signed by him showing that he was residing at the castle for a while in 1471. He was probably only passing through Penrith on his way from Carlisle, of which as Warden he also took charge, but his visits were most likely fairly frequent during the following years, and he may have stayed, as the plaque on the Gloucester Arms claims, at that house when it was Dockray Hall, though it was not the house that stands there now, which is Elizabethan. Nevertheless, one could not write about Penrith without acknowledging Gloucester's connection with the town, even if the people of Penrith have made more of it than was, in fact, true.

Gloucester was the son of the Duke of York, also called Richard, a great-grandson of Edward III, and Cecily Neville, known as 'the Rose of Raby'. He was born at Fotheringay Castle in Northamptonshire at a time of great unrest and impending civil war. His mother had been in her middle twenties when she married, which was late according to the custom of the time, and she had already borne her husband ten children, though only six had survived, when Richard came into the world on 2 October 1452. While Richard's elder brothers, Edward, Edmund and George, inherited something of their mother's grace and beauty, he did not do so. He did not enjoy good health as a child and seems to have inherited the dull features and stocky figure of his father.

When Richard was eight he and his brother George were attached to the household of Cardinal Bourchier, the Archbishop of Canterbury, at Lambeth and at Knole, in Kent. However, it was not very long before Richard, separated now from his brother, moved north to Middleham, in Wensleydale, to join the household of his cousin Warwick, the 'Kingmaker', whose daughters the boys were to marry. Richard spent most of his childhood at Middleham; he was what was known as a 'henchman', – that is, one who attended his lord riding on a 'hengst', a male horse, usually a gelding. At Middleham he had a chance to learn much that would stand him in good stead for the future, and to become friendly with the Earl's two daughters, Isabel and Anne, the younger of whom he would marry in 1472. Middleham, after Richard and Anne were married, was always their favourite home.

Richard was just eight years old when his father and brother Edmund, Earl of Rutland, were killed on the field at Wakefield. Soon his life changed dramatically, for within a year his brother Edward had become king, at the age of nineteen, and he himself had been created Duke of Gloucester and appointed Admiral of England. Richard's loyalty to his brother was constant. Unlike George, who had become Duke of Clarence and who rebelled against Edward, Richard stood by Edward in every crisis in the continuing conflict with the opposing Lancastrian party.

From the summer of 1471 until he came to the throne in 1483, Richard concentrated all his energy on governing the north of the country on behalf of his brother. Within weeks of the battle of Tewkesbury he was travelling towards the Scottish Border, where there was a renewed outbreak of unrest. Edward was determined that his eighteen-year-old brother should be rewarded with estates, but he was equally anxious to have someone he could trust in control of the north, and one whose military prowess would match that of the warlike Percy family. Now that the power of the Nevilles had been diminished, the balance of power might swing dangerously in the Percies' favour. Richard was to be trusted to carry out the 'King's work'.

Richard's headquarters were at Middleham, but he also inherited Sheriff Hutton and Penrith besides all Warwick's manors in Yorkshire and Cumberland. Edward also appointed him Warden of the West Marches towards Scotland and Steward of the Duchy of Lancaster.

Land and property were not all Richard stood to gain from Warwick's treachery and death, for in the summer of 1471 it was agreed that he should marry Warwick's younger daughter, Anne, who had been widowed when Henry VI's young son, Prince Edward, had been killed fleeing from the field at Tewkesbury. Anne had married the Prince when both of them were children, and it is exceedingly unlikely that the marriage was ever consummated. She was sixteen when she married Richard, and two years later she produced a son, another Edward. Everyone seemed happy except Richard's brother George, Duke of Clarence, husband of Warwick's elder daughter, Isabel. Clarence had opposed Richard's marriage out of greed for the rich Beauchamp estates that he coveted, but King Edward had come to the rescue with a compromise whereby the estates were divided between the two brothers, a situation that continued until Clarence's death in 1478. Isabel had died two years earlier.

Unexpectedly, in April 1483, the King died at the relatively early age of forty-one. He had left the throne to his son, Edward V, with the proviso that Richard should be 'Protector of the king and realm'. But the Queen, now the Queen Mother, was anxious to keep her influence over the boy, who was only 12½ years old, and above all her brother, Earl Rivers, and her son by her first marriage, Sir Richard Grey, were prepared to do anything to keep their new-found wealth and power by keeping close to the young sovereign.

The way in which Richard of Gloucester intercepted the King's party on its way to London at Stony Stratford and how he usurped the throne, imprisoning Edward and his brother, Richard Duke of York, in the Tower, and declaring the princes illegitimate because of the late King's bigamous marriage are well-known facts of history, or they have seemed well known until recently. Although some have challenged the evidence, it has been assumed that Richard was responsible for the two boys' death in the Tower, but in 1984 all the facts were argued out in a court case enacted for television viewers. *The Trial of Richard III* was no drama but a serious investigation into all the known facts, and the result was that Richard of Gloucester was found 'Not Guilty' of the Princes' murders. However, the fact remains that the little boys were never seen again, and it is incontestable that Richard ordered the execution of the Earl of Hastings, Lord Grey and Lord Rivers, though he was to look after his brother's wife well enough when she came out of the sanctuary from Westminster Abbey where she had taken refuge after Edward's death.

The problem, or rather the enigma, of Richard's character stems from the contrast between his 'evil' actions in the south, particularly after he usurped the throne, and the great good he did in the north, for the people of the north have always held him in affection. He brought peace to their region, and at Middleham he showed himself anxious to help the people by founding a college. In 1477 he had been granted by his brother a licence 'for erecting the church of Middleham into a college', where a dean and six secular priests were perpetually to offer Masses 'for the souls of his deceased relatives'. This looks like piety, but there is self-interest there too. As the guide to the church of St Mary and St Alkelda, at Middleham, says: 'One can only speculate on how Middleham and its collegiate church might have developed had not Richard been defeated and killed at Bosworth, in 1485.' One thing is strange: the college survived the Reformation and was not suppressed until 1845, by an Act of Parliament. There is a stained-glass window on the south wall of the church to Richard's memory, set there in 1934. The Richard III Society has been active since and in 1963 presented a green damask altar frontal to the church where Richard ensured Masses for his relatives – in particular he must have thought of his father and brother Edmund.

3

Market Penrith

'God's punishment in Pereth.'
Parish Register, 1597

In 1223 Henry III ordered the Sheriff of Cumberland as follows: 'Know that we desire that a market be held in our manor of Penred on the Wednesday of every week. And that a fair be held in the same place yearly, from the Eve of Pentecost, to last until the Monday next after the Feast of Holy Trinity.' Here was a Whitsun fair, if ever there was one, and the lord of the manor stood to make a healthy profit from the many stall-holders at both the market and the fair, but it was his responsibility to see that there was no unfair trading or forestalling. At Penrith fair there was what was known as a court of pie-powder, an emergency court that could try cases on the spot. The name comes originally from the Latin *pede pulverosus*, which in Norman French became *pied poudré*, meaning 'dusty-footed', and applied to any wayfarer or itinerant trader. The proclamation instituting the Penrith fair concluded: 'And if any difference should happen about any bargain, or any other matter relating to merchandise, thereupon proper notice shall be given to the steward, and the court of pie-powder shall immediately be summoned to settle the difference.'

The market charter of 1223 allowed Penrith to develop as a

market town, something it has remained ever since. Today, as in the case of many towns of a similar sort, it suffers from the constant flow of traffic through its centre, but this is not as bad as it was in the days before the opening of the M6 motorway in November 1968. The old North West Road, the A6, still passes through the market-place, and where the road narrows there is a necessary set of traffic lights to allow one-way traffic to pass between Devonshire Street and King Street. These 'Narrows', only some twelve feet wide, were once in competition with a street in St Albans as the narrowest on the route from London to Scotland.

As most people still feel the market-place to be the hub, if not the point of greatest hubbub, of Penrith, it is well to begin with it, but, as busy as it may be, it was a much more crowded place in the early years of the nineteenth century. Then one might have seen the Old Moot Hall, the Cross and Proclamation Stone, and the butchers' premises, the Shambles, as well as the large building known as the Roundabout.

The Cross was a small square building, with a roof supported by four square pillars, one on each angle of the steps, which was used as the butter and eggs market. It stood more or less where the Musgrave Monument now stands, and its roof provided a valuable shelter against the weather for the vendors, mostly women, who crowded there. Extending out from each pillar on either side were stalls made of stone; these were each five by 3½ feet and were let out to itinerant traders, who sold spices and many sorts of hardware. At the north-west corner of the Cross were the town stocks, concerning which there is an interesting record of 1781 to the effect that they were repaired by Thomas Lanhorne at a cost of £1.14s.

The Cross was also where the servants' hirings took place. A narrow roadway divided it from the shops on the east side, and between the Cross and the Moot Hall was a large flagged square called the Cross Parade. The whole area must have been crowded on Hiring Day, but at other times Cross Parade was used as a promenade and also as a place for games by the young people of the town. A subscription was raised to defray 'the expense of plastering the east wall of the Moot Hall, to have a smooth surface against which to throw their balls'. One cannot help thinking the adult population of Penrith must have been very considerate and tolerant in those days.

The Moot Hall stood on the north side of the square. It was built 'in place of the one that stood where Messrs Arnison's shop is now', partly of wood and partly of stone. The Hall faced the shops on the west side of the square and left only a narrow passage at the front and back. The back wall was much higher than the front, and the roof descended westward to form what was known as a 'teufa' – that is, a roof sloping one way only. At the front or west side, which bore the bear-and-ragged-staff coat of arms of the earls of Warwick, there were four or five small shops, and at the north end a set of stairs led to the great room, or assembly hall, in which the court leet and the courts incident to the manor and market were held.

On market day, originally a Tuesday, the Moot Hall was used as a market house 'where the country people, who spun a considerable portion of the wool they grew on their farms, brought their yarn for sale'. These truly 'home-spun yarns' were of two qualities, soft-spun and hard-spun, the former used for blankets and stockings, and the latter for coarser purposes. The principal buyers of this Penrith wool were the prosperous dealers from Kendal, as one would expect.

In a survey dated 1572 the 'Old Mote Hall' is mentioned as being held by one John Atkinson; this was presumably an earlier building on the same site which was replaced by the one I have just described.

From all accounts the Roundabout was more impressive than the Moot Hall. The building is shown in a drawing of Devonshire Street of about 1800, where its particularly large windows show that the Roundabout was a collection of shops. There were two shops on the first floor, while all round the building on the ground floor were butchers' premises 'protected from the rain by the pent roof which hung out aslope from the main wall'. The Roundabout was situated almost opposite the old Devonshire Inn, which was demolished in the early years of this century to allow the development of the Midland Bank.

Next to the Roundabout came two rows of Fish Stones, which, as their name suggests, were stone stalls on which fish were displayed. These were north of the Roundabout, as were the Old Shambles which extended as far as the King's Arms Passage; these were described as 'sheds with oaken rafters to hang joints upon'. It seems from early records that the Shambles were formerly situated in Burrowgate; perhaps they were considered unsuitably placed. I noticed when I was researching my book on Kendal that the Shambles there had shifted location three times, each time to achieve better drainage; perhaps Penrith had a similar problem, for it must be remembered that beasts were slaughtered and butchered in the streets. (The word 'shamble' is the Old English '*sceamol*' which meant a bench for the sale of meat, rather than a slaughter house, as is often supposed.)

J.E. Horsley in his *Jottings about Old-Time Penrith* published in 1926 mentioned that little meat was shown in Penrith market from Christmas to March, 'because the country people were in the habit of buying a supply at Christmas to pickle'. Mr Horsley also wrote of a small square building near the Moot Hall called the Balcony, 'on top of which was the market bell, and, underneath, a stall for the sale of meat occupied by Mr Thomas Carmalt'.

It has been assumed that the Cross, Moot Hall and Shambles were demolished before 1809. In the May of 1805 the Duke of Devonshire's agent reported that the Duke was 'diposed to meet the wishes of the men of Penrith, by consenting to remove the Old Shables'. About a year later another letter was received, which said: 'I think it would not be amiss if you could learn the sentiments of those whose property would be most benefited if the Moot Hall should be taken away, and what each of them would subscribe for purchasing a thoroughfare into Sandgate. If they do not come handsomely forward, I will advise the Duke either to build shops or sell it in building lots.' The subscription raised £431.3s.

In October 1809 a meeting of the Town Improvements Committee took place at the George Hotel 'to consult as to taking steps for the removal of the Roundabout'. The building was eventually sold for demolition on 27 May 1826. The bill of sale makes good reading: 'To be sold by public auction, in the Market Place, Penrith, on Saturday, the 27th day of May, 1826, at 7 o'clock in the evening, all the materials of the dwellinghouse known by the name of the Round-about, comprising the stone, timber, windows, lead, etc. The purchaser must take down and clear away the same in 10 days from the time of the sale, and pay the auction duty. Three months' credit on approved security. A discount allowed for ready money.' The auctioneer on that occasion was M. Thompson, and the bill of sale had been printed by James Shaw.

I have mentioned the stocks, but I have also seen several references to the town pillory that stood in the vicinity of the Cross. The whole market area was cobbled and remained so until the early 1900s. Altogether the market of the old days was a much more important occasion, when people had to travel by horse and cart or on foot to bring their goods to town. Today, the square is a busy main road, dominated by the Musgrave Monument, a clock tower described by Nikolaus Pevsner as 'utterly insignificant' – architecturally maybe, but it has become a familiar friend to to all who know and love Penrith, and sentimentally it is worth notice. On the north side the Monument bears the inscription: 'In sympathy with the great sorrow which befel the family at Eden Hall in the death of their eldest son, Philip Musgrave, on May 16th, 1859, at Madrid, in the 26th year of his age, this monument was erected May, 1861, a tribute from the town and neighbourhood of their high regard and esteem of Sir George and Lady Musgrave.' The Monument stands where the market-place merges with King Street, which on the north side gives access to the Old London Road and Friargate.

The Old Friary

As the name suggests, Friargate, 'the street of the Friars', takes us to the site of the old friary. Today, there is a house called the Friarage, but this was built long after the friars had left. All that remains of the old friary is a fragment of wall to be seen down an alleyway.

The friars settled in Penrith during the reign of Edward I, when soon after 1291, John de Capella granted some land in the town to the Augustinian friars of Newcastle-upon-Teyn. In 1299

Edward I gave alms to the Penrith friars who attended him on his journey south, so it is fairly certain that by then some of the Newcastle friars had settled in Penrith.

Friars were 'mendicant' – that is, they begged for alms and in theory lived off the voluntary donations of the faithful. However, they had to have somewhere to live, and as time went on they inherited certain properties. The friars at Penrith lived according to the Rule of St Augustine, as did the monks at Shap, but whereas the monks for the most part remained in the monastery, the friars would use their friary only as a base.

In 1350 the friars petitioned Bishop Welton of Carlisle to grant them a licence to 'officiate and perform divine service at Newton Reigny, which they alleged to have for some time destitute of a chaplain'. At this time, it seems, the friars were extremely poor. The same bishop granted an indulgence of forty days to all 'who should be present when the friars lighted their candles of Christmas Day, and to those who made them presents, because they were very poor'.

Many small gifts came the friars' way. In 1498 Robert Wrangwis, Fellow of Queen's College, Oxford, granted them lands in Penrith. It is thought that at the time of the Dissolution the friary possessed some four or five acres of land besides their buildings, but there is no record of what the friary was worth. In 1542 the whole property was granted to Robert Tyrwhitt of Kettilby, Lincoln. Walker's *History of Penrith* published in 1858 states that, 'The house in Friargate, still known as the Friary, occupies the site of the original edifice. When the trenches for the walls of the house called Abbott Bank were being dug, the ground floor of the chapel of the convent was discovered, and a quantity of human bones found under the chancel, including a pair of thigh bones of extraordinary size, and several undecayed skulls, with teeth still fresh and even.'

However many friars lay buried in the chapel, it is certain that any remaining alive in 1536 were forced to leave when the friary was dissolved. I have been unable to discover the exact date but assume it to have been some time before October 1536, when the people of Penrith joined what is known as 'the Pilgrimage of Grace'. The 'Pilgrimage' was, in fact, a rebellion, and the greatest challenge that Henry VIII faced during his reign. It had begun in Lincolnshire, but it spread quickly to the north across the Humber and was joined by thousands of men from the northern shires who demanded the restoration of the religion of their fathers which had survived in England for a thousand years. The rebels also demanded that new measures recently brought in should be revoked, particularly the closing of the small religious houses.

On 16 October a letter arrived in Penrith exhorting the people to swear an oath 'to be true to God, to the faith of the church, to our sovereign lord the King and to the commonwealth of his reign. And that having done that they should restore all the Abbeys suppressed.' The rebel leaders feared that unrest in the Penrith and Carlisle regions might provoke trouble with the Scots, so the letter ended with the advice that they should 'say such demeanour toward the Scot that no parade of war might ensue but all to be kept in good quiet and peace'.

By this time the Lincolnshire rebels had been dispersed without bloodshed, but the North was in a frenzy. The leader was a barrister called Robert Aske who was supported by many representatives of the great families in the north-east. Two brothers of the Earl of Northumberland, the heir to the earldom of Westmorland, five barons, twenty-three knights and twenty-seven gentlemen of the region attended the 'Pilgrims' Council' at Pontefract. Conspicuous by their absence, however, were Henry Clifford, Earl of Cumberland, and William, Lord Dacre. In Dacre's case it was understandable as he had only recently been released from the Tower after his trial for treason, and Cumberland left it to his son, Thomas Clifford, to join the rebellion.

The rebels were requested to take an oath on the Bible, 'the Oath of the Honourable Men', which spoke of 'purifying the nobility' and exhorted the rebels 'to expulse all villein blood and evil councillors against the commonwealth from his Grace and his Privy Council'. The rebels saw themselves as 'preserving the King's person' from heretic bishops, men like Cranmer, and scheming politicians such as Thomas Cromwell, of whom the men of Dent, in south Cumbria, said: 'If we had him here we would crum him and crum him so that he was never so crumwed.'

The people of south Westmorland marched down the Eden Valley towards Penrith led by Robert Thomson, the vicar of Brough. Thomson had been exhorted by his congregation to pray for the Pope of Rome, and the curate of Kirkby Stephen had been almost lynched for refusing to keep St Luke's Day as a holy day when the poor man had tried to implement a new royal edict suppressing various saints' days and holy days.

On both sides of the river the rebels came. On the west side Nicholas Musgrave led a group to Lowther; Penrith, as we have seen, had already joined the rebellion, and in answer to the entreaty of the Penrith leaders, Sir Edward Musgrave and the people of Edenhall came in on their side. Many from the Cumberland villages joined in. The tenants of Holme Cultram were particularly strong in number, but there were many from Greystoke, Skelton, Castle Sowerby and Hutton. On 24 October a Mass was offered in Penrith at which Robert Thomson preached a stirring homily on the Ten Commandments, in which he attempted to show how the present dilemma had been brought about by the people's neglect, for, as Aske was to say at his trial, 'The Abbeys in the north parts gave great alms to the poor men and laudably served God.'

While all this was going on, Robert Aske was in consultation with the Duke of Norfolk, the commander of the King's forces, at Doncaster. A truce was agreed. During the truce two representatives, Sir Ralph Ellerker and Robert Bowes, confronted the King at Windsor and put forward the rebels' demands.

The rising in the Penrith area met no opposition until the people reached Carlisle. There, Sir Thomas Clifford, promising to be the rebels' captain, was refused entry by the citizens. Thus thwarted, the rebels marched off to Cockermouth, where they were joined by the abbot of Holme Cultram. Such groups as these were assembling all over the northern counties when news of the truce arrived.

The King's answer came through the Duke of Norfolk on 6 December. He promised to pardon the rebels and call Parliament, and Norfolk, on his own initiative, it seems, promised that the monasteries would be restored, as a result of which the monks of Cartmel, recently suppressed, returned to their priory.

The truce was abided by on the east coast, but here in the west there was to be more trouble, which suited the King's plan. The Document of Pardon had been drawn up with convenient loopholes. In this added disturbance tithe barns were burned down, and no gentlemen were admitted to the council of the rebels as they could not be trusted. Beginning in Westmorland, with particular unrest in the Appleby and Kirkby Stephen areas, the movement spread to Penrith and Cockermouth. On 16 February, some six thousand men mustered on Broadfield Moor intending to attack Carlisle, but they were grossly disorganized and soon fled when Sir Christopher Dacre came on the scene with five hundred spearmen.

In such disarray the rebellion came to an end. Terrible reprisals were to follow, for the King claimed that the unrest had begun outside the period of the truce. The principal leaders, including Aske, were executed. Forty-five Westmorland men were hanged in chains in their villages '*pour encourage les autres*', their bodies left to weather and rot and picked by ravens and crows. In Cumberland twenty-one suffered a similar fate, among whom were William Bunting of Greystoke and Robert Goodale and Lancelot Richardson of Newton; from the town of Penrith there eight men: Thomas Burtbeck, Edward Whitelock, John Stephenson, Michael Grey, William Stephenson, Sir Edward Penrith, a priest, and Edward Stephenson.

With such suffering did the people of Penrith witness the 'going of the friars' in 1536, and the rotting corpses of their leaders provided a sordid reminder of what might happen to those who resisted the authority of the second of the Tudor kings.

Penrith and the Plague

The Chronicles of Lanercost Priory record three epidemics between the years 1201 and 1346, and it is known that there had been a recent outbreak of the plague when St Cuthbert preached in Carlisle in 685. Although evidence is lacking, it is reasonable to assume great loss of life in the main outbreak, nationwide, of

1346. The Scots became victims to the disease in 1380 when they made a surprise attack on the town at the time of the annual fair.

The word 'plague' originally meant any epidemic with a high mortality rate, though it later came to be applied exclusively to the bubonic and pneumonic forms that killed something between a third and a half of the population of Europe and which was known as 'the Black Death'. The bacillus that caused the plague, *pasteurella pestis*, was only identified in 1894. The germ breeds in rats, who suffer even more severely than humans, and it is transmitted from them to humans by fleas. Of the two forms the bubonic plague is relatively uninfectious, since the disease is fought out in the local swellings. The pneumonic form, however, is lethal and highly infectious, affecting the lungs and usually resulting in a swift death. In the sixteenth century Penrith was struck by two outbreaks of plague; the first, in 1554, affected Kendal as greatly as Penrith, but it was nothing like as serious as the one that came forty years later.

The years 1597 and 1598 were catastrophic for the town, with an outbreak of plague that carried off something like a third of the inhabitants. The pestilence had, according to tradition, entered the town from the north-east; originating at the port of Newcastle, it struck the little village of Kirkoswald and spread southwards to Penrith and thence to Appleby and Kendal.

The records of deaths in the parish register are prefixed with the stern words: 'God's punishment in Pereth', and the parish of St Andrews recorded 583 deaths. The inscription in the church recording 2,260 deaths refers to the outlying parishes in the district as well; even so, it is a staggering number.

The disease is thought to have been brought to the town by Andrew Hodgson, described as a foreigner – what today would be called an 'offcomer', one not native to the place. Hodgson was lodging in a house in the corn market and succumbed to the plague towards the end of the third week in September. He was buried on the 22nd. By the second week in October the Railton family had become infected, and five members of the family had died by 5 November. Five days later the first member of the Hewer family died, and three others died in a fortnight. The

Devonshire Street – Penrith

FREEMAN HARDY WILLIS

Long Meg and her daughters

The Eden at Temple Sowerby

St Andrew's Churchyard – Penrith

Cornmarket – Penrith

Penrith – ancient and modern

The ways divide – Albert Street, Penrith

A corner of Old Penrith – Little Dockray

Shap Abbey

incubation period was anything from a week to ten days, but once the symptoms became apparent, the third and fifth days were those of the greatest danger. On the third day the bubo, an inflamed swelling of the glands in the groin or armpits, appeared; on the fifth the febrile symptoms began to abate; if the patient survived the fifth day, and the bubo was fully formed, the patient could be considered out of danger.

During the autumn and winter of 1597 the disease spread relatively slowly, and, though shocked, the people of Penrith seem to have carried on their lives fairly normally – for example, the parish register shows that the Sacrament of Matrimony was administered at the usual rate.

However, by the early summer the plague renewed with increasing intensity, so that on 29 May thirteen people died. The disease was no respecter of persons, and Lancelot Musgrave of Musgrave Hall, Middlegate, succumbed early in the same months.

In his *History of Penrith* Walker describes the feelings of the people in a fine prose passage which I will not attempt to surpass:

> During this dreadful time, the actual state of Penrith can scarcely be imagined. Not a solitary marriage is registered for the whole summer. Houses supposed to have caught the infection were shunned, and their inmates suffered to die unaided. People almost feared each other's looks. Evening, the time when the attacks of this disease generally come on, has peculiar terrors during a visitation of the plague. The first paroxysm or period, which included from the evening to the close of the following night, is frequently fatal. All these circumstances are only too well known where the plague has been for some time raging. The wild and furious look accompanying the disease in its incipient state, which should bespeak pity for the sufferer, dispels all feeling of humanity from the breast of those whom chance brings in his way. The staggering occasioned by an extreme prostration of strength, is a warning to his neighbour to flee. The poor sufferer seeks his home, – perhaps the last of his household, – and the indifference to recovery, which is considered a most unfavourable symptom, alone relieves the horrors of his despairing and forlorn condition.

Understandably, the people from the neighbouring villages

gave Penrith a wide berth, and many, it is said, would not venture nearer than Pooley Bridge. For the short period there was no central market, and by tradition there were smaller markets held at each end of the town, including one at the north-east end in a street originally known as Grub Street but later becoming Milton Street. Here, according to Walker, a stone, 'something like a market cross', remained to point out the site for many years, but it was removed when the ground was taken over by buildings. The other temporary market was held at the south-east end of the town where today the Plague Stone remains as a reminder of the time. This block of freestone has a small hollowed-out centre, ten inches deep and about twelve inches square. It is thought to have contained vinegar in which coinage was disinfected at the time of the plague.

Only a small percentage of those who died during the epidemic could be buried in the churchyard; some were interred in the schoolhouse yard, while others, the majority, were buried in a mass grave out on the fell. One record speaks sadly of 'a poor boy unknown, who was buried on the fell'.

During the summer and autumn of 1598 the epidemic raged. On 11 August the parish register records seventeen deaths; on 2 September twenty-two persons died. The onset of winter brought an abatement to the disease, and the last person to die of this plague, Margaret Winder, succumbed on 6 January 1599.

Life slowly returned to normal, and more people had the courage to risk marriage: eighteen marriages were solemnized in a matter of a few weeks, whereas none had taken place during the summer of the previous year. The vicar of Penrith, whose wife had died in the epidemic together with his son, took as his wife Dorothea Machell, as Walker remarks, 'setting a striking example to his honest parishioners'.

Perhaps news of the weakened state of the people had reached the ears of the Scottish marauders, for in March 1600 there took place a 'great spoiling, robbing and burning' throughout the county. But the Scots could hardly instil such fear as was caused by the plague, and the people of Penrith might well echo the words of Petrarch who, describing the devastation of the town of Florence by the Black Death, wrote: 'O happy posterity, who will not experience such abysmal woe and will look upon our testimony as a fable.'

Sandgate

Sandgate is a large square on the north-east side of the town centre. It is linked with Friargate by De Whelpdale Lane at its southerly point and by Benson Row a little further north. Visitors to the town who have travelled by bus will know Sandgate well enough, for the bus station is situated at the northern side of the square, though formerly the buses used to congregate in the square itself.

Not very much of old Sandgate remains beyond Sandgate Hall, built in 1646. The Hall has been modernized and converted into three dwellings, but it was for many years the town house of the Fletcher family, owners of Hutton in the Forest, and their coat of arms is on the ceiling of the cottage at the corner.

Sandgate gained its name from the sandy bottom and edges of the beck that once ran through the square, and in its well-constructed culvert it does still run, of course. It is thought that the square was originally designed 'to provide a place of refuge for the peasants and cattle from outlying areas at the time of the plundering forays from over the Border'. (We shall meet this use of a square surrounded by houses at several places, particularly at Milburn and Askham.)

Not only was the annual fair held at Sandgate, but bulls were baited there until the practice was declared illegal in the 1820s. Up to that time all beef sold in the town was 'baited beef', and indeed it was illegal to sell any other kind without advertising the fact. It was thought that the flesh of an angry bull was more tender to eat than that of a docile one, something we in this country, thank God, are now unable to judge. There is a drawing by Thomas Fawcett showing the hounds baiting a bull in Kirkby Stephen market square in about 1817, and the last bull was baited in Appleby in 1812, a few years after it had been officially banned in Westmorland. Such scenes would have been a familiar sight to the people of Penrith also, and the Sandgate led conveniently into Burrowgate, where, as I have said, the Shambles were once situated.

Burrowgate and Sandgate are probably the oldest streets in Penrith, and both are mentioned in documents dated 1298. The 'Burghgate' is simply 'the town street', and the name gives us no problem of meaning, unlike the other large square of the town, Great Dockray. There are several places with this name in Cumberland: a Dockray Nook in Lamplugh, and Dockrays in Matterdale and Woodside. The 'ray' part is simple enough; it is the Old Norse '*(v)ra*' meaning a nook or corner and often used to describe a secluded place. It is found in Wreay, Wrayside and numerous other field-names in the area, sometimes hidden, as in Lacra and Murrah. The 'Dock' part is almost certainly the Old English '*docce*', according to the English Place-Name Society, but there is also the Norse word '*dokke*' meaning a 'hollow', which seems more likely and could refer to the area below the hill on which the castle is situated.

Great Dockray is approached from the market-place principally by way of the corn market, though there are numerous other possible approaches. The name still exists as a reminder of the many facets of Penrith's market activity, but also mentioned in the eighteenth century are the following; the barley market, the horse market, the oat market, known as the haver market from the Old norse word '*hafri*' meaning oats, the beast market and the wheat market, and the wool market was mentioned in 1619. Most of these are marked on the map included in *A Survey of the Lakes of Cumberland, Westmorland and Lancashire* by J. Clarke, which shows that the different sorts of grain were sold at particular areas of the corn market and were associated with particular inn signs, barley at the sign of the Griffin, wheat at the Black Lion and so on.

Great Dockray is not strictly speaking a square, but it is probably the best looking of the Penrith market 'squares'. I have already mentioned Dockray Hall, now the Gloucester Arms, in connection with Richard of Gloucester. At the south end of Great Dockray is the Two Lions Hotel, which was once the town house of Gerald Lowther, built in 1585. Inside there is a particularly fine decorated plaster ceiling, which is well worth seeing.

One of the features of modern Penrith is the covered market situated at the point where Cornmarket meets Great Dockray.

This was erected in 1983 and, with nearby Poet's Walk, has added lustre to the old town, preserving moderately good taste in each case.

This chapter on the market will end away from the hubbub of commerce. Near the George Hotel, once the Old George and dragon, is a way through to St Andrew's churchyard and, as it were, another town.

To come off the busy main streets into St Andrew's churchyard is to step into another century. A wide footpath separates the houses which surround the close from the graveyard, which in turn is encircled by railings. The houses are almost all fine and, except for the older Tudor House, may all be summed up in the word 'Georgian'.

The church at the centre is, as Nikolaus Pevsner noticed, 'the stateliest church of its time in the county'. There has been a church on the site since very early times, but there is no record until Henry I granted the advowson of St Andrew's, Penrith, to the Bishop of Carlisle in 1133. Only the west tower of an earlier church was implemented into the church built between the years 1720 and 1722. The building is of the familiar sandstone and hardly prepares one for what is inside, for the body of the church has three galleries on Tuscan columns; entered by a two-armed staircase in the west tower is another gallery, from which the three-tier galleries may be reached.

From the ceiling hang two giant brass chandeliers, which were presented by the Duke of Portland to the people of Penrith for their part in resisting the Jacobite Rebellion of 1745. Among the many interesting features in the church are the stained-glass portraits of the Neville family in the window in the south aisle. These are said to be portraits of Cecily Neville and Richard, Duke of York, but are now considered to depict Cicely Neville's parents, Ralph Neville and Joan Beaufort, since drawings showing the full figures were discovered.

In the chancel there are two paintings by Jacob Thompson, *The Agony in the Garden* and *The Angels appearing to the Shepherds*, painted in 1845.

Perhaps at this point it might be apposite to say a little more about the Duke of Portland, who donated the chandeliers, since his name lives on in the town in Portland Place. Portland was a Dutchman, Hans Willem Bentinck, a particular favourite of William of Orange. In 1675 Bentinck had slept in William's bed to attempt to 'draw off' an attack of smallpox, and there could hardly be a better act of friendship than that. When Bentinck accompanied William to England in 1688, he and his wife, Anne Villiers, continued to be the King and Queen's closest friends, and for his loyalty Bentinck was showered with honours, being created Duke of Portland and granted valuable estates in Wales and many parts of England, including the Honour of Penrith in Cumberland. This grant of property in Cumberland gave the Bentincks great influence over the succeeding years. Their struggle with the Lowthers, and their defeat, resulted in the Cumberland property being sold to the Duke of Devonshire, which is why Penrith also has a Devonshire Street.

The Giant's Grave

One of the 'musts' for visitors to Penrith is an inspection of the 'Giant's Grave' and the 'Giant's Thumb' in the churchyard. Two Anglian crosses and four hogs'-back tombstones form what is called the 'Giant's Grave', and a tall standing stone at the north side of the main entrance is the 'Giant's Thumb'. At one time the grave was thought to be that of Owen Caesarius, King of Cumbria, who died in about 937, but the crosses are unlikely to have been placed on a grave in this way. They are undoubtedly Christian, and on the east cross of the grave there is an Agnus Dei carved above a serpent, and below, a woman and a bound man:

> Adam lay y-bounden
>   Bounden in a bond;
> Four thousand winter
>   Thought he not too long;
> And all was for an apple
>   An apple that he took,
> As clerkes finden written
>   In theire book.
>
> Ne had the apple taken been,

The apple taken been,
Ne hadde never our Lady
A been heaven's queen.
Blessed be the time
That apple taken was!
Therefore we may singen
'*Deo Gratias!*'

4

A Poet in Town

'March 11th. – Mrs. Wordsworth, wife of John Wordsworth, Esq., of Cockermouth, aged 30. Buried.'

Penrith parish register, 1778

Penrith would not claim to be in the same league as Cockermouth or Grasmere for the part it played in the life of William Wordsworth, but it is very proud to boast a close relationship, for the poet's maternal grandparents, the Cooksons, ran a mercer's business in a tall house that stood beside the old Moot Hall. There is a plaque recording the fact set into the wall of Arnison's shop, though it is misleading since the present building was erected much later on the site of the Cooksons' house.

William Cookson had married Dorothy, the daughter of Christopher Crackenthorpe, of Newbiggin Hall. Wordsworth's mother, Anne Cookson, was born on 20 January 1745, an ominous year for the town, when the streets were crowded with Scottish troops in support of the Young Pretender. It was in Penrith that Anne Cookson met her future husband, John Wordsworth, whose father, Richard, was a lawyer and land agent cum farmer from Sockbridge, about three miles east of the town. After serving his apprenticeship, John Wordsworth was appointed steward to the Whitehaven part of Sir James Lowther's estate and moved to Cockermouth. On 25 February 1766 his marriage to Anne took place in Penrith parish church, and the couple took up residence in the large house in the broad main street of Cockermouth which Sir James Lowther had bought for his representative in West Cumberland. It was there that Anne later gave birth to her five children, the eldest, Richard, being followed by William, on 7 April 1770, and Dorothy, on Christmas Day 1771. It was in the parish church at Penrith that William and Dorothy were baptized on the same day, 18 January 1772. Why so long had elapsed before William was baptized is a question that has not been answered.

As their father was so industriously employed guarding Sir James's interests (something he was to do right up to his death in 1783), the Wordsworth children were often taken to their grandparents by their mother, and the years 1776 and 1777 were largely spent there, Anne having by that time produced two more sons, John and Christopher.

From their grandparents' home in Borrowgate, William and Dorothy attended Anne Birkett's dame school in St Andrew's churchyard. Mrs Birkett took the children up on to Beacon Hill to roll their pace-eggs at Easter-tide, and on May Morning Dorothy was encouraged to bring her doll to school to be hung from the school window in garlands of flowers with the other girls' dolls. One of these other girls was little Mary Hutchinson, whom many years later William would marry and whose father ran a tobacconist's shop in the town. William was to recall many details of their childhood: 'We had practised reading and spelling under the same old dame at Penrith, a remarkable personage, who had taught three generations, of the upper classes principally, of the town of Penrith and its neighbourhood.'

As idyllic as life at Ann Birkett's school seemed for the young Wordsworths and Hutchinsons, sadness was to come early in the Wordsworth family when Anne Wordsworth died at the age of thirty. She had caught a chill while on a rare visit to London and on her return to Cockermouth had become so ill that she broke off her journey at her parents' home and died a few days later.

She was laid to rest in Penrith churchyard on 11 March 1778 (the site of her grave is unknown).

'I remember my mother only in some few situations,' Wordsworth recalled, 'one of which was her pinning a nosegay to my breast when I was going to say the catechism in the church, as was customary at Easter.' His last impression was 'having a glimpse of her on passing the door of her bedroom during her last illness, when she was reclining in her easy chair'.

Of all her children, Anne Wordsworth had been most anxious about William: his future, she felt, would be remarkable 'either for good or for ill'. 'The cause of this was, that I was of a stiff, moody and violent temper,' he later admitted, 'so much so that I remember going once into the attics of my grandfather's house at Penrith, upon some indignity having been put upon me, with an intention of destroying myself with one of the foils which I knew was kept there. I took the foil in my hand but my heart failed.' It is odd to think that the heart that leapt to the rainbow might have been thus stilled!

William Wordsworth was to spend much time in Penrith during his vacations from Hawkshead School and, later, from Cambridge. It was in the town that he was to nurse his friend Raisley Calvert, and we get a glimpse of him later in life, in 1823, when he attended a ball in the town with his daughter, Dora. Dora remembered that, 'Father was the gayest of the gay in spite of his eyes – made agreeables to every lady in the ballroom, and notwithstanding the lights was all the better for the exertion.' This was the last time, as far as is known, that Wordsworth was in Penrith.

Another Wordsworth link in the town is the town hall, which stands in Stricklandgate, but this time it is the poet's cousin, John Wordsworth, who died in 1819, who is remembered. Two houses built in the Adam style (what Pevsner calls 'Adamish', for it is highly unlikely that Robert Adam himself designed them) had been erected in 1791. One of them was known in the town as Wordsworth House before the pair were converted into the present town hall in 1906. A local architect, J. Knewstubb, began the work in 1905 and at the cost of £7,000 completed the conversion, conserving only two chimneypieces of the original houses on the exterior but preserving several features inside, particularly the staircase and the fireplace in the front entrance.

The town hall stands in close proximity to the street that has several of Penrith's most interesting historical features, Middlegate.

Middlegate

Devonshire Street leads into Middlegate, in 1551 written as 'Medilgate', the middle street. All the 'gates' appearing in Penrith street-names come from the Old Norse '*gata*' meaning a road and should not be confused with any sense of an entrance.

On the west side of this street one sees something of the small yards that were once such a feature of the town. These were nothing like as extensive as the yards in Kendal but they served much the same purpose in keeping houses closely in touch with one another in times of danger, and often members of the same trade would keep together, weavers, tailors tanners and the like. It has been suggested that the inscription which includes a pair of shears and the date 1697 over the doorway leading into Williamson's Yard may mean that there were wood-staplers occupying the yard. A reasonable assumption.

Where Middlegate meets Brunswick Road there stands a large house, Musgrave Hall, once the home of the Musgraves of Eden Hall. On the opposite side of the road is a low building dated 1670 which today houses the Tourist Information Centre and a small display of museum exhibits. This is Robinson's School, erected by public subscription and taking its name from its most liberal benefactor, William Robinson, a native of Penrith who left in his will, 'issuing and paying out of his premises in Grub Street, London', the sum of £20 a year for ever, for the education of poor girls. The girls were to be taught 'reading and seamstry work, or such other learning fit for that sex, being the poor sort whose parents were not able to pay for their learning'. The bequest was to the vicar and churchwardens of the parish church and was dated 1660.

In 1700 the parish made regulations for the government of the school, by which the mistress was required 'to teach all children that are sent unto her by the minister and church wardens, gratis, without demanding any reward.' The school was to receive numerous endowments subsequently in money and in gifts. Mrs Bland, who had been a mistress at the school, left four Bibles, with the Act of Uniformity, the Book of Common Prayer and the Apocrypha.

In 1860 there were seven schools, besides the grammar school, in the town: the Spinning and Knitting School, a branch of Robinson's; the Boys National School, which was founded in 1816 in Benson Street; the Infant School, founded in 1828; the Wesleyan Day School, in Meeting House Lane, founded in 1844; the British School, built in 1847, in Canny Croft, and what was called a Ragged School which commenced at the Town Head in 1853.

The standard of education in Cumberland and Westmorland during the eighteenth and nineteenth centuries was consistently high. After his years at Hawkshead Wordsworth found when he reached Cambridge that his knowledge of mathematics was greater than that of many young men from the south. Perhaps Hawkshead was exceptional, for it is known that boys from as far away as Edinburgh attended the school. It had been founded by Edwin Sandys, Archbishop of York, in Queen Elizabeth's reign, in 1585, which is some nineteen years after the great school in Penrith, Queen Elizabeth's, was founded.

Queen Elizabeth Grammar School

Penrith is justly proud of its grammar school, whose character was granted in 1564 by Elizabeth I, but it was not the earliest school in the town. In 1340 John de Eskehevod was licensed by the Bishop of Carlisle to teach the art of grammar, and in 1361 Robert de Burgham was similarly licensed to teach the 'psalter, Priscinius's Grammar and singing'. In 1395 Bishop Stickland founded a chantry in the parish church in honour of St Andrew. The chantry priest's duties, besides offering Masses for the souls of the faithful departed, included the teaching of church music and grammar. When the chantry was dissolved in 1547, during the reign of Edward VI, the people of Penrith were educationally impoverished, and they eventually petitioned Queen Elizabeth to grant them a school. The charter was granted under the title of the 'Free Grammar School of Queen Elizabeth in Penrith' and was dated 18 July 1564.

The charter makes interesting reading. We should not be surprised to learn that the lands which formerly had produced the stipend for the chantry priest were 'now or lately in the possession of Richard Lother Knight'. The intention of the school's foundation was 'for the instruction of boys and youths in grammar'. There was to be 'one master or teacher and one usher or under-teacher', a situation which was 'to continue for ever'. The charter also stipulated that, in order

> That our intention aforesaid may have the better effect, and that the lands and tenements and other things to be granted, assigned and appointed for the maintenance of the school may be better regained for the continuance of the same school, we do will and order that hereafter and henceforth, for ever, there be and shall be within the town and parish of Penrith in the County of Cumberland, five of the more discreet and upright men of the same town and parish, for the time being, who shall be and shall be called the Governors of the possessions, revenues and goods of the said school.

The first 'discreet and upright men' to be appointed governors were Richard Dudley of Yanwath, Thomas Carleton, Anthony Hutton, Nicholas Boast and John Whelpdale, and the first master of the school was John Davis, who took up his appointment in 1569. Davis remained at Penrith for some seven years before moving on to become master of the school at Blencow.

The scholars had to be at the school by six in the morning, and they remained at school for twelve hours. There were frequent prayer sessions interspersed between the lessons. They were taught music and the catechism. In 1607 it was recorded that all or most of the school books had been lost. Obstinate boys were to be expelled, and twice a year the master was to 'certify all incapable boys'. No foreigners were to be received.

In 1706 the vicar of Penrith, Dr Hugh Todd, and the governors issued a set of school rules which were 'Extraceted out of the Laws of the Land, the Canons of the Church, and the original Charter of the said School'. The master was to be a person of liberal education, well skilled in the Greek and Latin languages: and, 'if it conveniently can be so, in some Degree in Schools, in One of the Universities'. He was to be licensed by the bishop of the diocese and 'shew his conformity to the Doctrine and Discipline of the Established Church, according to the Acts of Uniformity'. Rule VI insisted that the master should see that his pupils knelt and stood in the proper places during the divine service and answer 'Amen' and make other responses. Rule VII required that the master should report to the diocese all boys of 'Pregnant parts and laudable inclinations to Learning' so that, with 'Diocesan Incouragement' and their parents' and friends' assistance, they might be 'serviceable in some more than ordinary degree either in Church or State'. To which end, one supposes, Rule VIII might be necessary, namely, that: 'The Master and Usher so form the Speech and Language of all their scholars, by constant and frequent Exercise, that they may speak with a Clear, Audible and Distinct Voice.'

Such were the general rules laid down, but the 'Particular' rules give such a fascinating picture of life at the school that they are worth much fuller quotation:

I That All the Scholars of the said School now Admitted, or hereafter to be Admitted, shall comport & behave themselves Religiously and Dutifully toward God; as becometh those who partake of a Religious and Liberal Education.

II That All the Scholars shall behave themselves Dutifully, Orderly & Soberly, toward their Superiors, Equalls and Inferiors. That they pay all due Respect to the Governors of the School, and to the Master and usher; Submitting themselves to their Orders and Admonitions willingly and readily. That they converse quietly and amicably with One another: never quarrelling or fighting: never slandering, cheating or defrauding: much less Swearing or Cursing or Lying in their Conversation, under due and severe punishments, to be ordered by the Master or the Governors.

III That in their Sports and Recreations, the Scholars Converse, and Sort with One Another: and avoid the Company of Prentices & Idle Boys, and all such as are of ill Qualities and Reputation, that they be not tainted and infected by their bad Conditions.

IV That All the Scholars of the School, be divided or Distributed into 4.5.6.7. or more Classes, Seats or Forms; according to their Number and Proficiency; And that the Master have a General Care of All; but a particular Regard to the 5. or 6. First or Highest Seats or Classes: Leaving the Inferiors or Parvulars to the Direction and Attendance of the Usher.

V That Every Scholar, Living or Boarded within the Town come diligently and constantly to School, at Six a clock in the Morning, while Bell rings, or presently after, both Summer and Winter. That they be allowed to go to their Breakfast at half an hour after Eight. That they return to School at Nine; and continue there till Twelve or near to it; and then to be dismissed to their Dinners. That at One a Clock All return to School, and remain there Studiously and orderly, till six at night. And this Rule and Order to be Observed during the whole year.

VI That Public Prayers be said in the School by the Master, or in his Absence, by the Usher, Morning and Night; in English; as shall be allowed and directed by the Rt Worsp. the Governors.

VII That every Sunday and Holiday, at Eight in the Morning, every Scholar repair to School to be Catechised and Ordered as the Master shall direct.

VIII That there be two Monitors in the School, and that the Scholars in their turns take care of the Keys, that belong to the School doors, and ring the Bell immediately after the Clock has Chim'd Six, or get some to do that Duty for them.

IX That no Scholar reveal or tell abroad, what is done in the School: not Sollicit any Gentleman to get play upon pain of rendering themselves lyable to such Corrections as may be justly due to them for their Rudeness in so doing.

X That the four last Classes constantly speak Latin One to another, both in school and at Play & that notice be taken of those, who transgress this Order.

XI That no Scholar presume to play in the Church-yard, Streets or other public Plaeces. But that they divert themselves at their innocent Recreations in the Fields, Bishops Yards and such like Places.

XII That according to the Customs of the best Schools, there be allowed to the Scholars at the Great Festivals of the Year,

Spaces & Times of Vacation & and Remission from their Studies.

XIII That that rude Custom of barring out the Master, and taking violent Possession of the School be utterly abolished and laid aside; as is already done in All Schools of better note & and a more improved discipline. That the usual Contributions be continued; and that the Scholars be allowed one Day every year in memory of their former Privilege.

XIV That there be kept in the School one Baculum or Clogg: And that one go out of the School but by leave first asked of the Master or Usher: And that they go only then, two at a time & and return in less than a Quarter of an hour, and always take the Baculum with them.

XV That whosoever shall break the School or Church windows or do any damage to what belongs to the Public, Shall make good the Loss and Damage, & also be punished for the Fault.

XVI That every Scholar (especially those of the upper Classes) in the Families where they Live & reside, be regular & and exempliary in their Behaviour: That they Observe and Practise private Prayers and Devotions.

XVII That every Scholar (as much as possible) go handsome, neat and clean in their Apparel; behave themselves mannerly and civilly towards All: And especially pay all Dutiful respect to the Governors and principal inhabitants of the Town.

XVIII That the Scholars do not Suffer any noxious Creatures, or filthy Skins, or the like to be, or be hung up in or near the School, or Church-yard, to the Prejudice of their Health.

XIX That if any Scholar Shall Absent himself from School without a just cause; or if Any Shall refuse Submission to such Punishments as his misbehaviour may deserve, the Governors be informed of it, & the Truant or Rebel be expelled the School.

XX That the Scholars do not Suffer idle Boys to play in the Church-yard, or near the School, or Church at School hours; to the disturbance of their Studies, by their Noise and bad Example: But if any such be found, to have them brought within the School-gate & there whipped, at the Discretion of the Usher.

This set of rules was signed, as were the general rules, by Dr Todd, the vicar of Penrith, and three governors, Richard Hutton, John Pattenson and James Pearson, and dated 1 September 1708.

Penrith school was one of twelve in Yorkshire, Cumberland and Westmorland which had the right to send a candidate every five years to Queen's College, Oxford, to compete for one of the five exhibitions bequeathed by Lady Elizabeth Hastings. However, the relationship of the three counties with the college had begun very much earlier, when in 1340 Robert de Egglesfield founded the college as a compliment to the wife of Edward III, Philippa of Hainault, to whom he was confessor. Besides being the Queen's chaplain, Egglesfield was also vicar of Brough: hence the connection. Many boys who began their education in the small village schools went on to become Fellows of Queen's College and to reach even higher distinction, such as Edmund Gibson, of Bampton, of whom I shall write in the next chapter, Christopher Bainbridge, of Hilton, who became Archbishop of York and a cardinal, and Thomas Fothergill of my own parish, Ravenstonedale, who became Provost of the college and Vice-Chancellor of the university.

In 1857 the old school building was replaced by another on the same site. It may still be seen near the main entrance to the church.

The Particular Rules had made several references to the churchyard, and the boys were warned against 'obnoxious creatures and filthy skins, or the like' that might endanger health, but there were times when the yard in front of the school was also used for burials, especially during the plague, and for this purpose 'and for the portion of the school yard permanently enclosed within the churchyard, the school received an annual payment from the churchwardens of 15s'.

Today the grammar school is still flourishing at its spacious premises on the Ullswater Road. The move took place in 1915, when the neo-Georgian main building with a cupola designed by Harrison and Ash was completed. Judging by my several visits to the school to speak to the sixth form, it seems destined to go from strength to strength. Of course, the school is now co-educational, but in the days before girls could attend there were several private girls' schools in the town, for instance, Portland House in Wordsworth Street, Brunswick House in Brunswick Square, and Mrs Fletcher and Mrs Horn's separate Young Ladies's Schools, in Arthur Street.

Each religious denomination had its own school. The Wesleyans, as I have mentioned, opened a school in 1844, and the Catholics founded a school in 1882, situated in Drovers' Lane on the opposite side of the road from the church dedicated to St Catherine. The church had been built some thirty years previously in the Gothic style from money donated by several people but particularly by Lady Catherine Throgmorton, to whom there is a commemorative stained-glass window facing south-west, designed by Francis Barnett of Edinburgh.

Also close by is Penrith's second Anglican church, Christ Church, which was consecrated in 1850; William Holme Milner was the first vicar.

Middlegate leads northward into Duke Street, and Duke Street into Stricklandgate, named after Bishop Strickland, unlike the Stricklandgate in Kendal which takes its name from the family in general. Stricklandgate leads in turn into Scotland Road as it rises uphill towards the turning to Great Salkeld. At the bottom of the hill where the two roads meet are Foster Street and the house, Page Hall, where Thomas Plimsoll and his family lived between 1828 and 1838. Of the five Plimsoll children, Samuel, the fourth, was to achieve fame as a member of Parliament and particularly with regard to shipping and all its problems which led to the Shipping Act of 1879 and the introduction of what came to be called 'the Plimsoll mark' painted round the sides of merchant vessels.

Samuel Plimsoll was born in Bristol on 10 February 1824, and he was therefore four years old when his father moved to Penrith. The family attended the services at the old Ebenezer Chapel, known locally as 'the Beck Side Chapel' but in 1865 replaced by the Congregational chapel, which is now the United Reformed church. It is thought that Samuel Plimsoll received his early education from a curate attached to the chapel. He remained a staunch Congregationalist all his life, though, it was said, he was 'equally attached to all denominations of evangelical Christianity'.

Plimsoll held radical political views and eventually entered Parliament as M.P. for Derby. But he is best remembered for the famous Plimsoll Mark, his reference to 'Coffin Ships' and the rubber-soled shoes that still bear his name.

Another famous name that Penrith may justly claim as its own is that of John MacAdam. He moved to Cockell House, a good-looking residence built in 1750 and situated in Drover's Lane, some time in 1820. At around this time he published his *Present State of Road-Making* which went into five editions in two years and established his name in the public mind.

5

The Vale of Lowther

Lowther! in thy majestic Pile are seen
Cathedral pomp and grace, in apt accord
William Wordsworth, 1831

The River Lowther rises on the northern slopes of the Shap Fells. From the fastnesses of Brown Howe, Saddle Crags and Sleddale Pike, fells some 550 metres high, small streams or 'sikes' race northward towards Sleddale Beck, which skidaddles on down between Todcrags and Tongue Rigg only to be frustrated in that journey by the great barrier that allows the waters to rise, flooding the valley to form Wet Sleddale Reservoir and to reach a healthy height for the benefit ultimately of Manchester. It all seems something of an anti-climax, particularly if, as I have been assured, much of the water, having reached its Mancunian destination, is immediately pumped back in the direction from whence it came. From the damn sluice the River Lowther, now bearing that name, begins its northerly way which takes it through the old Abbey Park and the sad ruins of Shap Abbey. By Bampton much swelled by the waters of Swindale and Haweswater Becks, the river reaches Askham, leaving the shell of Lowther Castle on its western side, and on by Clifton towards Eamont Bridge. But suddenly the Lowther veers eastwards, flowing on for a further mile to join the River Eamont by even more ruins, those of Brougham Castle.

The small hamlet of Wet Sleddale was described by Dr Burn in 1777 as a place where, 'If rain is stirring, the air scoops it surprisingly into the hollow of that dale.' What Dr Burn could not have foreseen was that the dale would become completely soaked by the Manchester Corporation Waterworks. Today the reservoir is in the good hands of the North West Water Board.

'Sleddale' means a valley, and in the fullest sense, since the Old English '*slead*' and the Old Norse '*dale*' mean the same thing. This is a typical example of the needless repetition noticeable in several Westmorland place-names. This particular Sleddale is designated 'Wet' to distinguish it from the neighbouring Longsleddale through which the River Sprint flows on its curving, southerly course towards the River Kent and Kendal. Yet 'wet' it is, and a Manchester Corporation Waterworks brochure once informed its readers that the average rainfall in the dale was seventy-four inches compared with the national average of forty-four inches!

On the north-west side of the valley were Sleddale Hall and Sleddale Grange, the latter originally one of the granges of Shap Abbey. In 1360 several persons 'committing several disorders' broke into the Grange and other houses in the area belonging to the abbey. The bishop issued a mandate to the vicar of Shap and neighbouring clergy to denounce the offenders with the 'great excommunication of bell, book and candle', which meant that the offenders would be outlawed. But the record remains a mystery, for it is not known what the offence was, though it seems most likely to have been some form of witchcraft judging by the punishment.

There is a small photograph of the door-lintel of the Grange in the Westmorland Inventory issued by the Royal Commission on Historical Monuments in 1936 showing the stone inscribed with the initials RMN and the date 1691. John F. Curwen noted that the place became at one time 'a pretentious dwelling', which adds to its mystery; nevertheless, the Grange seems to have had a more interesting history than the nearby Hall.

The Lowther then leaves this attractive reservoir behind and takes its northerly course to Thornship and Keld. I did not notice anything particularly 'foamy' about the river, but the origin of the name seems to be the 'foamy' or 'lathery' river. Perhaps the flooding of Wet Sleddale and the resulting slowing down of the water-flow by the dam have altered the river's nature. Thornship is really 'Thorn-shap', a small hamlet three-quarters of a mile south-west of Shap village. It is said that there was at one time a large oak tree 'planted on the top of the hill for the direction of travellers' known as the Shap Thorn. This was described in 1851 as 'recently cut down', but no explanation has been offered as to why an oak should be called a thorn.

Keld, 'the spring', is well known locally for its chapel, which was presented to the National Trust by Sir Samuel Scott in 1918. The chapel is a simple building, 'plain and oblong', and thought to date back to the fifteenth century, though the three-light east window looks later than that. About 1650 the chapel was occupied as a dwelling house, and in 1890 it was described as 'the ruins of a small chapel which serves as a cow-house'. It has risen somewhat in the world since then.

Keld is reached by a narrow road from Shap village and is situated where the Lowther begins a westward curve through the ancient Abbey Park and the site of the Abbey Mill through Abbey Wood towards the ruins of the abbey itself.

Shap Abbey

What is left of Westmorland's only abbey is well worth a visit. The ruins are particularly well cared for and well marked out. The abbey, dedicated to St Mary Magdalene, was built by the Premonstratensian canons over a period of many years, but its foundation was at an uncertain date towards the end of the twelfth century, at any rate before 1170, when Brampton Church was appropriated to the abbey.

The original choice for a foundation site had been at Preston Patrick in the Kendal Ward, but the position was considered unsatisfactory.

The Premonstratensian Order was founded in 1121 by St Norbert, who built an abbey at Prémontré, near Laon, in France, on the spot revealed to him by the Blessed Virgin Mary in a vision: hence the name, which means 'shown before'. The priests, who were canons, strictly speaking, as opposed to monks, followed the rule, so-called, of St Augustine. (This 'rule' from the Latin '*regula*', was nothing like as comprehensive as the rule St Benedict set down for his monks.) The canons of Prémontré became known as Norbertines after their founder, and as 'White Canons' because they wore a white woollen habit. The order grew rapidly, and after only thirty years there were some hundred abbeys, many of which were situated in England and Scotland. The first English house, at Newhouse, in Lincolnshire, was founded in 1143. Newhouse founded another abbey at Croxton, in Leicestershire, and from Croxton was founded Cockersand Abbey on the mouth of the River Lune: this was in 1190. Croxton also founded Blanchland, in Northumberland, in 1165, and Preston Patrick was the first stopping place of the community that would move to the Lowther Valley and establish themselves at Shap Although owing its origin to Blanchland, it was soon decided that Cockersand, being much closer, should become the mother-house, and in this connection it is interesting that Thomas, son of Gospatrick, was one of Cockersand's first benefactors. Perhaps at the time Blanchland had more men to spare – we shall never know, and indeed there is not very much known about the abbey's history because, as the official guidebook notes, 'Nearly all its records have been lost.' What is known is that the canons worked in several parishes in the neighbourhood, at Shap itself and Bampton, but also further a field, at Warcop and at Appleby, where they ran the leper hospital.

Among the many abbots of Shap, one rose to considerable eminence in the Church: this was Richard Redman, whose family owned Levens Hall, near Kendal. Redman was appointed Bishop of St Asaph in 1471 by Edward VI. In 1496 he became Bishop of Exeter, and six years later Bishop of Ely. Up to the time he died in 1505 Redman remained abbot of Shap, and it was during his abbacy that the great west tower was built on to the abbey church, and well built too, for it still dominates the ruins and gives some idea of how splendid the church must have been. The north transept was standing when S. and N. Buck drew the ruins in 1739, and in the possession of the Society of Antiquaries there is a pen-and-ink drawing of 1859 which shows clearly the nave piers.

Shap Abbey was dissolved relatively late. On 14 January 1540 the last abbot handed over the abbey's property and possessions to the Crown agents and was compensated by a pension of £40 a year, with smaller sums allotted to the canons. The land was sold to Sir Thomas Wharton, who did surprisingly well out of the spoliation. As governor of Carlisle Castle, he was in a position to be able to purchase manors from the Tudor government, and he was a particular favourite, having risen from a fairly humble position in the Percy household to become Sheriff of Cumberland and Member of Parliament for Appleby. By 1532 Wharton was Justice of the Peace for Northumberland, Cumberland and Westmorland, and after the Pilgrimage of Grace, in which he was ruthless in his part of the reprisals, in 1537, he was appointed Warden of the West Marches. In this position he led the attack against the Scots at the Battle of Solway Moss in 1542, for which service he was given a barony. He remained Warden until 1559, some ten years before he died. Into the hands of this ambitious and ruthless man came much that the religious orders had nursed through the centuries, all that the canons had worked for at Shap and the similar endeavours of the Gilbertine canons at Ravenstonedale.

All seemed well for the Whartons, but eventually Thomas Wharton's descendant, Philip, first Duke of Wharton, rebelled against the Hanoverian Succession, joined the Jacobites and was disgraced, dying in Spain at the early age of thirty-two, in the care of the Bernardine fathers. The wheel seemed to have come full circle: all Wharton's estates were forfeited, including the properties that had once belonged to Shap Abbey and all the first Lord Wharton's manors. Most, if not all, easily slipped into other – one might even say equally grasping – hands, for the Wharton properties were snapped up by the Lowthers, who will come to dominate the rest of this chapter. However, before the Lowthers begin enclosing, building and destroying villages, let us look at the village of Shap itself.

Shap

The earliest records speak of 'Hep' or 'Heppe', and the village's name has the same origin as the word 'heap' and seems to refer to the ruins of an important megalithic monument (lying on the main road up Shap Fell about a mile south of the village, or, as it was always denoted, the town): a long line of stones, of which Goggleby Stone and Thumder Stone are part. Camden noticed 'several huge stones standing in a row for nearly a mile'. In 1775 Lady Lowther made a drawing of the monument showing a stone avenue. Nothing as comprehensive or as observable as that remains.

Why the 'H' sound should have changed to an 'Sh' is rather a complicated matter of phonology and arises, as the phonologists say, 'from stress-shifting in the diphthong and the substitution of Sh for Hy'. It has also happened in the case of Shipton in Yorkshire.

The parish of Shap originally contained four townships, Mardale, Shap, Shap Rural and Thornthwaite. At the mention of the name one may imagine that Shap Rural covered a wide area, and indeed it did.

The village of Shap has developed along the main road, the A6, and, inasmuch as it is still flourishing, it has a much longer history than the abbey, though the village was always served by the abbey, and one of the canons was parish priest at the church.

The manor of Shap belonged from ancient times to the Culwen (later spelt 'Curwen') family, who held it under the Cliffords, the lords of the barony of Westmorland. It is recorded that Sir Gilbert de Culwen released the manor to Shap Abbey in 1360, during the reign of Edward III. It seems that only part of the manor was then held by the abbey, for in 1422 it appears to have been owned jointly by the abbey and Christopher Curwen, but very soon the Curwens allowed the abbey to lease it all.

Considering its position along an important highway and the fact that there was a church in the 'town' as early as the thirteenth century, there is very little known about the history of Shap village – perhaps its records, like those of the abbey, have been lost. Shap was never a mediaeval market town, as were Orton and Kirkby Stephen. Its market charter was granted as late as 1687, when Philip, Lord Wharton, obtained a charter to hold a Wednesday market and three fairs a year. Later the weekly market was held on a Monday in a building erected at the expense of William, Earl of Lonsdale, in 1861, while fairs were held on 25 January for horses, cattle and sheep, on the third Monday in March for cattle and sheep, and on 4 May for horses, cattle and sheep.

Market House is to be seen half-way down the village street. This was the earliest market building and was erected some time in the 1690s. It has three by three bays, with round arches on stout little columns, while on the upper floor the small round-arched windows have been filled in. Today it is in good use as the Shap branch of the Cumbria County library.

The life of Shap village changed dramatically when the M6 motorway was opened, and the main street which for so long had been on the main road to Scotland became relatively quiet. However, one may see from the number of inns that still open that Shap was developed as a 'stopping-place'. Familiar names remain, such as the Greyhound, the King's Arms, the Crown and, at the north end of the street, the Bull. Shap is also one of the few small villages to possess its own bakery, whose baking is of a particularly high standard.

St Michael's Church is set up on a small hill, above and to the east of the main street. It is largely a reconstruction carried out in 1898 to 1899, although the west tower had been built slightly earlier, in 1828. However, there has been a church on the site since the thirteenth century, and part of the south arcade includes four bays, 'round piers with the simplest round capitals', which were in the original church built in about 1200.

In the churchyard there is a memorial to the men who died working on the Lancaster to Carlisle Railway; it is dated September 1846 and situated at the right of the main entrance gates. The workmen, or navvies, who worked on this stretch of the line were English mostly, unlike those on the stretch north of Penrith who were predominantly Irish. On one occasion on 11 February 1846, the Westmorland and Cumberland Yeomanry Cavalry had to be brought in to restore order and clear the Penrith streets of rioting navvies. This was the second time such measures were necessary in Penrith, the former occasion being the Chartist Riots in the May of 1839.

At the north end of Shap village a road leads off westward back towards the Lowther; passing Skellaw Hill and the lane that leads down to the abbey, it turns north-westerly and then runs more or less parallel with the river towards Rosgill. Unexpectedly Rosgill means 'the ravine of the horses' and comes from the Old Norse '*hross*'. Although part of Shap parish, Rosgill was a separate manor and was held by a family that took its name from it. During the reign of Henry III a John de Rosgill was a witness to a grant of land at Thrimby; later a de Rosgill brought the manor into the Salkeld family's possession. The Salkelds owned Corby Castle and held on to Rosgill until 1631, when Dorothy, sister of Richard Salkeld, brought it in marriage to the Christians of Unerigg, in Cumberland, by whom it was eventually sold, like so much else in the area, to the Lowthers.

At Rosgill the Lowther is spanned by a bridge about which there are several interesting records. In July 1697 the people of Rosgill complained that the bridge was very much in decay 'and that by reason of its being only a wooden construction and subject to many hazards by the great inundation of waters and a continual charge upon the county in repairing the same'. At the same time it was decided to seek an estimate as to the price of building a stone structure. Eventually a stone bridge is spoken of, though by 1756 this too was in a bad state of repair. In June 1887 two foals jumped over the parapet wall into the river twelve feet below, and one of them was killed, while cattle jostling to cross the narrow seven-foot bridge were 'pushed over by the others and sheep very frequently'. Today the bridge looks sturdy enough and means that the next village, Bampton, may be approached from either side of the river.

Bampton

Although there is no church at Mardale, Bampton is linked to it, forming a united benefice. The link is not new, for part of the chapelry of Mardale was always part of Bampton parish, while the other part was in Shap Parish.

From earliest times, from the twelfth century at least, records show that Bampton consisted of three distinct manors: Thornthwaite, often referred to as Bampton Patrick, taking the name of Patrick de Culwen, an early owner; Bampton Carhullan, where there was a stone circle at Towtop Kirk, and Bampton Cundale, named after the Cundale family.

Bampton came into the possession of the Curwens in 1392 but soon seems to have become associated with the Cliburns; from them it came to the Warwick family, who sold it in 1772 to Edward Hasell of Dalemain. The Hasells then sold it to the Lowthers, so that the three manors of Bampton became part of 'Lowtherland'.

The River Lowther divides Bampton into two small villages, Bampton Grange, where the parish church is situated with the inn, the Crown and Mitre, and Bampton itself on the west side.

The parish church dedicated to St Patrick was largely restored in 1885, but this was the restoration of the church built between the years 1726 and 1728, not the earlier church which had been served from the abbey. There was probably a church at Bampton in Anglian times, and we know that in 1170, the year of St Thomas à Becket's murder, the church here was appropriated to Shap Abbey. This was confirmed in 1263, by the Bishop of Carlisle, who granted to the abbot and convent, in consequence of the smallness of the revenues of that establishment, the privilege of officiating in the said church 'by two or three of their own canons, one of whom to be presented to the bishop as vicar, to be answerable to the bishop in spirituals, and another to be answerable to the abbot and convent in temporals. They were, however, bound to have one secular chaplain in the said church, to hear confessions and execute other such matters as could not be so properly done by their own regular canons.'

In 1362 the vicar, John de Askeby, bequeathed his body to be interred in the choir of the church. If, as seems fairly certain, the present building was raised on the foundations of the old, the good vicar's bones must rest there still.

On the walls of the church inside are several memorials and two good paintings in oils, one, on the north wall, of the Reverend John Bowstead by James Ward and the other, on the west wall, of Bishop Gibson by the Dutch artist Johan van der Branck. These seem to me the most interesting features in the church.

Edmund Gibson was born at Bampton in 1670 and left the school there at the age of sixteen to go up to Queen's College,

Oxford, where he distinguished himself. It is thought his knowledge of local place-names and dialect came in useful at a time when a study of the northern languages was particularly cultivated in Oxford. Gibson translated the *Chronicon Saxonicum* into Latin and published it himself, together with the Old English original and his own learned notes. Later he published two editions of Camden's *Britannia* and in 1698 brought out an edition of *Reliquiae Spelmanianae*, the posthumous works of Sir Henry Spelman, relating to the laws and antiquities of England, with a life of the author. The work was dedicated to Archbishop Tenison, later spelt Tennyson, to whom Gibson became domestic chaplain. The Archbishop gave him speedy preferment, appointing him rector of Lambeth and archdeacon of Surrey.

So thorough was Gibson's knowledge of the law, both civil and ecclesiastical, that it was at one time thought that he studied for the bar before ordination. This seems not to have been the case but in 1713 his most important work, *Codex Juris Ecclesiastici Angliani*, ensured his fame. In 1715 Gibson was appointed Bishop of Lincoln, and in 1720 he became Bishop of London. In the House of Lords he stoutly opposed the repeal of the Test and Corporation Acts and a bill for the relief of Quakers as regards tithes. It is said he was a 'bitter enemy of religious equality' but that he approved of the toleration of Dissenters. He preached boldly against the foolery and masquerades at the Court of George I and even presented an address to the King to abolish all Court entertainment. The old puritan died at Bath on 6 September 1748, at the age of seventy-nine.

Bishop Gibson was not the only eminent churchman to be born at Bampton, for he was preceded by Hugh Curwen, Archbishop of Dublin and Lord Chancellor of Ireland, said to have been born in Bampton Patrick in about 1500. Like the Vicar of Bray in the song, Curwen changed his allegiance according to the times; ordained a Catholic priest, he seems to have had strong Protestant leanings during the reign of Henry VIII, accepting royal supremacy and preaching in favour of the King's marriage to Anne Boleyn. During the short reign of Edward VI it is recorded that Curwen accepted the Book of Common Prayer as readily as he had done the missal at his ordination. However, he returned to Catholicism during Mary's reign and indeed owed his consecration as archbishop to the Queen; the ceremony was held on the Feast of the Immaculate Conception 1555, 'with all the pomp of the Roman Pontifical'. When Elizabeth succeeded to the throne, Curwen accepted the Settlement and was translated to the see of Oxford in 1567. He died at Swinbroke, near Barford, the following year.

There is no record of where Curwen received his early education, prior to going up to Brasenose College, Oxford. The school that Bishop Gibson had attended was founded in 1623 by the Reverend D. Sutton, vicar of St Saviour's, Southwark, who was a native of Bampton. The Free Grammar School was to be placed under the management of twelve governors, of whom the head of the house of Lowther was always to be one. According to the institutes framed in 1665, the schoolmaster was required to be 'in holy orders, and a licensed preacher'. John Bowstead, the master whose painting hangs on the wall of the church, was at the school for fifty-six years. He was a fine teacher and was said to have 'educated more students for the Church than any other man in England'. It was Bowstead's boast that he had 'eddicated three hundert preests'.

As the River Lowther continues northward on its journey, it passes the small hamlet of Helton to the west and the vast area of Lowther Park to the east. The Lowther Wild Life Park is well known to thousands of people, for it is a very popular playground in the summer months, with its Adventure Playground, the many different species of wild animals, and the herd of deer that grazes among the well-established trees. Among these trees it is not unusual to see macaws flying from branch to branch, though these are perhaps not seen as frequently as the macaws in Kirkby Stephen which often fly in from Eden Place, where John Strutt has some sixty tropical birds flying free.

Lowther Park was the setting for Lowther Castle, the ancestral home of the earls of Lonsdale. As I have said, the castle itself is now the mere shell of a ruin, but in its heyday it was celebrated for its somewhat 'flashy' grandeur. The castle, completed in

1811, was built to plans prepared by Sir Robert Smirke, a young architect recommended to the Lowthers by Sir George Beaumont. However, as the history of the Lowthers goes back a very long way, Smirke was relatively late on the scene.

The Lowthers

The Lowther family claims its origin among the Danish invaders who came in their longboats during the ninth century, a colourful beginning, and in many respects the family has been 'colourful' ever since, – I am not just referring to the bright Lonsdale yellow, common to every AA car and relay truck that we see on the motorway.

However far the Lowther claim may reach back into the remote past, the first members of the family to appear in records are William and Thomas de Lowther, who appear as witnesses to a grant in the reign of Henry II; but what might be called the 'regular pedigree' commences in the reign of Edward I. From that time onwards there is no doubt about the important role the family has played in the history of Cumberland and Westmorland. Time after time a Lowther is listed as Knight of the Shire, or High Sheriff; Sir Hugh Lowther fought at Agincourt in 1515; Sir Richard de Lowther befriended Mary, Queen of Scots; the list of the family's achievements is impressive by any standards.

The first Lowther to be knighted by the sovereign was the John who was dubbed by Charles I; but it was not until the Glorious Revolution, so-called, of 1689, that the Lowthers were raised to the peerage. For his part in securing Carlisle and the two counties for 'King Billy', Sir John Lowther became Vice-Chamberlain of the Royal Household, a Member of the Privy Council, Baron Lowther of Lowther and, in 1696, Viscount Lowther; it was he who began to develop the ancient family home at Lowther into a mansion.

Early in the seventeenth century there was nothing but a pele tower three storeys high, a hall, a large bedroom and what were described as 'several low old rooms', but when Celia Fiennes visited Lowther in 1698 she saw the new Hall that Sir John had had built at a cost of £7,000. She wrote: 'I went to it through fine woods, the front is just facing the great road from Kendal and looks very nobly, with several rows of trees which leads to large iron gates, open bars, into the stable yard which is a fine building on the one side of the house very uniform, and just against it is such another row of buildings the other side of the house like two wings which is the offices; its built each like a fine house jutting out at each end and the middle is with pillars white and carvings like the entrance of a building.' Such were the stables and offices, but the house itself, she noticed, had a flat roof and was built of 'the red sort of stone of the country'. The garden steps and statues were limestone: 'four little Cupids or little boys in each corner of four squares'. Celia Fiennes takes great care to describe the decorations in several of the rooms. Here is her description of the noble, very lofty hall: 'The top and sides are exquisitely painted by the best hand in England which did the painting at Windsor.' The painter was Antonio Verrio, and he had depicted 'gods and goddesses that are sitting at some great feast and a great tribunal before them, each corner is the seasons of the year with the variety of weather, rains and rainbows, stormy winds, sun-shine, snow and frost with multitudes of other fancies and varieties'. It all looked, she noted, very natural: 'It cost £500 that room alone.'

The Hall was badly damaged by fire in 1720, but although Robert Adam submitted plans for a castle-like mansion in 1767, nothing was done until the early years of the next century. By then something had happened in the Lowther family that was to be of great importance, for the different Lowther estates had become united when in 1751 James Lowther, of Maulds Meaburn, inherited both the Lowther and the Whitehaven estates and the title from two cousins.

James Lowther was born in 1736, the second son of Robert Lowther of Maulds Meaburn who had become Governor of Barbados. He succeeded to the baronetcy in 1751 on the death of Henry, third Viscount Lowther, and in 1755 his cousin Sir James Lowther left him all the accumulated wealth of the Whitehaven branch of the family.

In 1757 the young Sir James, described as 'ruthless, able and ambitious', sat in Parliament for Cumberland, at the beginning of a long career. He married Lady Mary Stuart, the eldest daughter of the third Marquis of Bute. Although the marriage was a failure, when his wife died Lowther is said to have preserved her body in a glass-lidded coffin so that he could gaze at her fondly. Surely this alone would have been sufficient grounds for nicknaming him 'Wicked Jimmy' but a Whitehaven man who offended him was press-ganged into the navy and made to serve for ten years, and de Quincey told of Lowther's terrifying carriage drives through the small Cumbrian villages, so that folk would close the shutters in fear of being bewitched.

Perhaps 'Wicked Jimmy' is best known for having introduced the younger William Pitt to the House of Commons as member for Appleby. Lowther controlled Appleby as one of the nine seats known as 'Lowther's Nine-pins' and he was prevailed upon to give Pitt his chance there. Pitt had been a Cambridge friend of the Duke of Rutland, who, unable to obtain a seat for him, begged Lowther to put him in for one of his boroughs. There is a curious tale told in Wraxell's *Memoires*. The go-between between the Duke and Lowther was a man named Kirkpatrick, from Penrith, who was a protégé of Sir James and was well known in Newmarket where the Duke considered him a buffoon. One morning in the autumn of 1780, the Duke sent Kirkpatrick to Sir James, whom the messenger found shaving.

'Well, Kirk,' said Sir James, 'what may be your business?'

'I come from Arlington Street with a message from the Duke. He requests that you will oblige him by reserving a seat for a friend of his, Mr Pitt, Lord Chatham's brother, a gentleman of vast abilities, whom the Duke wishes to bring to Parliament.'

'I wish he had sent sooner to me,' said Sir James. 'Is he very anxious about it, Kirk?'

'Extremely so, you may be assured.'

Sir James saw the Duke, and in consequence Pitt was put up for Appleby, for which place, and Carlisle, Sir James Lowther himself had been returned, but he had elected to sit for Carlisle. Pitt represented the borough from 1781 to 1784.

For his services to Parliament Lowther was created Baron Lowther of Lowther, Lord of the Barony of Kendal, Lord of the Barony of Burgh, Viscount Lonsdale, Viscount Lowther and Earl of Lonsdale. This was on 24 May 1788, but some years later, in 1797, further honours were conferred upon him, and the titles of Viscount and Baron Lowther of Whitehaven were added to the already long list. Lord Lonsdale died at Lowther Hall at the age of sixty-five in 1802 and was buried at Lowther.

His death was a blessing for the Wordsworth family, for the poet's father, whom we have seen was his agent, had died being owed a considerable sum of money in back pay, and sums he had lent his master had never been repaid. The situation was made good by Lonsdale's heir, William Lowther, the son of a clergyman from Swillington, who became first earl of a second creation. It was he who employed the services of Robert Smirke to change the burnt-out ruins of Lowther Hall into a magnificent castle, which when completed was considered the finest of houses to visit.

Smirke was not Lowther's first choice of architect. Plans were drawn up by Webster, of Kendal, and Harrison, of Chester, and some work by Webster was begun at Lowther in 1803; in the same year George Dance, Surveyor to the City of London, visited Lowther but, finding the distance too far at his age (he was then in his sixties), decided to recommend Smirke. Smirke arrived on the scene in April of 1806 and completed his work in 1814. In the September 1821 issue of the *Lonsdale Magazine* there appeared a description of the castle: 'Nothing can be imagined more strikingly beautiful than this assemblage of towers. The graduation in height is so pleasing and the intermingling of the numerous turrets so picturesque that nothing could be added to increase its magnificence, nor anything omitted without impairing its beauty.' Lowther and Eastnor Castles were the finest examples of Smirke's earlier work. In pseudo-Gothic style, they are not, however, typical of his work as a whole, and he seldom used the style in later life, preferring to use classical forms instead. In 1823 he commenced work on his two finest buildings, the General Post Office in St Martin's-le-Grand and the British Museum. His other important commissions were the east wing of Somerset House, the London Custom House, the College of Physicians in Trafalgar Square, the Carlton Club, which was later rebuilt and the Union Club; with his brother,

Sidney he designed the Oxford and Cambridge Club in 1856.

Smirke was knighted in 1832.

Of the earls of Lonsdale who are associated with the 'glory' of Lowther, none has captured the imagination as did the fifth Earl, the celebrated 'Yellow Earl'.

Hugh Lowther was born in London on 25 January 1857, the second son of Henry Lowther, who would later succeed to the Lonsdale title as the third Earl. His mother was Emily, daughter of St George Francis Caulfield of Donamon, Roscommon. He was sent to Eton, but thoughts of an academic nature never entered his head; by the time he was nine he had become an accomplished horseman and, it is said, was up at the kill 'when the field had been reduced to four' on his first hunt. This was a good omen for one who became in turn master of the Woodland, Pytchley, Blankney, Quorn and Cottesmore hounds. One cannot help wondering what Hugh Lowther would have made of the hunt saboteurs, but he gave 'personal chastisement' to a countryman who had run over and killed a hound.

As a young man Hugh Lowther toured with a circus in Switzerland, spent an extraordinary year in the Arctic and had the distinction of confirming the presence of gold in the Klondike. An expert all his life on all aspects of hunting, a lover of the turf, though winning only one classic race, the St Leger, in 1922, Lowther also became well known in boxing circles, and the Lonsdale Belts of the National Sporting Club have linked his name with the sport to this day.

A great yachtsmen, he raced Kaiser Wilhelm's crack cutter *Meteor* and won seventeen prizes in twenty-two races; he remained a close friend of the Kaiser, refusing to renounce his friendship after the outbreak of the First World War, much to his credit. There was always a bust of the Kaiser in a place of honour at Lowther, which the Emperor had visited in 1895 after the Cowes Regatta. In his life of Hugh Lowther, entitled *The Yellow Earl*, Douglas Sutherland describes the visit:

> For months before the actual date of the visit Westmorland and Cumberland had been in a state of turmoil. The police forces of the two counties had been combed in an effort to ensure that all the best looking and most athletic members of the force were temporarily

> drafted to Penrith for route lining and crowd control duties. The hunt servants of the Quorn, in full hunting kit, were sent up to Lowther to ride behind the Kaiser's carriage, and the whole of the Westmorland and Cumberland Yeomanry devoted months to ceremonial drilling and kit polishing in the hope of being one of the two hundred to be selected for the honour of acting as Lord Lonsdale's household cavalry for the duration of the visit. An enthusiastic gossip writer of the time remarked, 'Lord Lonsdale is in very truth a prince in his own country.'

It was the individualist in Lonsdale which made him the idol of the Victorian and Edwardian populace, his side-whiskers, his gardenia buttonhole and his nine-inch cigar. When he drove to the royal enclosure at Ascot, his wagonette in yellow and black and his perfectly matching chestnut horses, with the grooms and postillions in their yellow Lonsdale livery, he was the envy of the nobles and the star of the people.

The Lonsdale yellow was adopted by the Automobile Association when Lonsdale became its President in 1907. Today, it is less noticeable, since both British Rail and British Telecom have adopted a similar shade, but in its heyday it was as distinctive as pillar-box red.

From 1917 to 1944 Lord Lonsdale was Lord Lieutenant of Cumberland, though he spent less time in the county than he did at his home, Barley Thorpe, in Rutland. He had married Lady Grace Gordon, the sister of the Marquis of Huntly, in 1878, but the couple had no children. Lady Lonsdale died in 1941, three years before her husband, who died at Stud House, Barley Thorpe, on 13 April 1944. He was succeeded by his brother Lancelot, who died in 1953.

The present Earl of Lonsdale lives at Askham Hall, the early home of the Sandford family, and a late seventeenth-century reconstruction and development of a fourteenth-century pele that itself had been transformed into a mansion in 1574.

At about the time Charles II was dying, in 1685, there was great activity at Lowther, when Sir John Lowther pulled down the old village and began the building of Lowther New Town. These houses stand east of the lawn and avenue between the castle ruin and the church, near the Victorian-looking estate offices.

St Michael's Church situated north of the castle is largely a reconstruction built in 1856, but there are incorporated into it many features of the almost total rebuilding by Sir John Lowther in 1686. However, there has been a church on this site since the twelfth century, and part of the north arcade is of that date, while the central tower is of the fourteenth century.

Inside there are many Lowther memorials, tablets and sarcophagi, and outside in the churchyard stands the Lowther Mausoleum, which houses the lonely, seated figure of William, second Earl, sculptured by E.B. Stephens in 1863, some years before his subjects death. There is little here to suggest 'The marble index of a mind for ever/Voyaging through strange seas of thought, alone'. The Lowthers have never been quite like that. In the words of Hugh Lowther's famous toast: 'The Queen, the ladies and fox-hunting.'

Askham

Lowther church stands on a small rise, and this is a good vantage point from which to view the river at its best. A good footpath follows the river to Clifton, but I shall cross over and continue towards Askham, one of the most attractive villages in north Westmorland. Askham is the place 'at the ash trees'. The manor was acquired by Sir Thomas de Hellbeck in 1280, but it passed by marriage to the Swynburn family in 1314. It was the Swynburns who constructed the first defensive building on the site of the present Hall. When in 1375 the manor passed to the Sandfords, in the person of Edmund de Sandford, there began an association with that family that lasted for some 350 years. At one time the Hall had a private chapel dedicated to the Blessed Virgin Mary, which was described as being in use as a dairy in 1910. When Askham became part of the Lowther Estate, the hall became the rectory for Lowther parish, though, as I have said, it is now the home of the Earl of Lonsdale.

Within the boundary of Askham parish there are many early settlements, several stone circles and earthworks. These are situated west of the village and are of particular interest at Moor Divock and on Skirsgill Hill, where there are two settlements of the 'British' type together with traces of walls, banks and an extensive lynchet system, in all covering some thirty acres.

Hackthorpe

Hackthorpe is situated on the east side of Lowther Park, and it is the last place we shall look at before we allow the Lowther to speed off northwards towards Eamont Bridge. Hackthorpe is one of the townships of Lowther but was a manor in its own right in the reign of Henry III, when 'Ralph de Aincourt released to William de Lancaster and his heirs his right in fifty shillings of land, in which he was bound to him by the charter of William de Lancaster, his grandfather, for the quit claim, which the said William made to the same Ralph, of the service of Gamel de Hackthorpe'. Gamel was released 'in drainage and other service'. In 1361 Sir Thomas de Strickland was granted a licence from the Crown to impark his woods at Hackthorpe and other places, for his good service in France. Strickland held Hackthorpe under the barons of Kendal, for, as we shall see, several manors in the area were part of the Kendal barony, in spite of their being so close to the Appleby barony of the Cliffords. The stricklands were to sell their interest in Hackthorpe to the Lowthers in 1525.

Hackthorpe is 'Haki's hamlet' and must therefore have had an early Norse owner, though nothing is known of him. The village is a mile and a quarter from Lowther Castle and five miles south-south-east of Penrith, and the A6 passes right through it. On the west side of the road, slightly apart from the main group of houses and to the south of them, is Hackthorpe Hall. This particularly good-looking house was built by Sir Christopher Lowther in the reign of James I; it contains two oak-panelled bedrooms, in one of which was born Sir John Lowther, who became MP for Westmorland and 'distinguished himself in the cause of William and Mary by seizing in Workington harbour a ship which was laden with arms for the garrison at Carlisle, then in the hands of King James II'.

It was at Hackthorpe, in a cottage called 'The Hermitage' which Lord Lonsdale had presented to him in 1844, that the artist Jacob Thompson spent the last years of his life.

He was born in Penrith in 1806, the son of a Quaker factory-owner in the town. In spite of his nonconformity, Jacob

Thompson was educated at the Queen Elizabeth Grammar School. When he left school, his hopes of being apprenticed to Charles Thurnham, the Carlisle printer, were not fulfilled, and he worked as a grocer for a time before being apprenticed to a Penrith coach-painter. In those days as an apprentice Thompson learnt to apply paint to houses, signboards and coaches, and after two years he decided to set up a business of his own. In 1824 something happened that was to change his whole life: a visit to the Carlisle Academy Exhibition so impressed him that he decided to take up landscape painting, and the following year he was himself an exhibitor.

Thompson attracted the attention of the Earl of Lonsdale, who employed him to copy paintings hanging in Lowther Castle. It was one of these copies sent to Sir Thomas Lawrence that resulted in Thompson's moving to London in 1829, where he studied under Henry Sass and attended life classes at the British Museum, before becoming a student at the Royal Academy. It was none other than Robert Smirke who advised him to 'guard his originality' and leave the school. Thompson became a regular exhibitor at the Royal Academy Exhibitions, and after 1844 he remained in Westmorland.

It is by paintings like *Drawing the Net at Hawes Water*, of 1867, and *The Rush Bearers*, of 1872, that he will be best remembered, besides the paintings in St Andrew's, Penrith, which replaced earlier murals by Matthias Read.

Jacob Thompson died at the Hermitage in 1879, and he lies buried in the churchyard at Lowther.

6

Dacre of the North

'All the north is ready and only awaits the release of the Queen of Scotland.'

Guerau de Spes, 1568

The River Eamont may hardly be said to 'rise': it flows from the north-easterly tip of Ullswater. After two miles or so it is joined by the waters of Dacre Beck and continues to meander for another twelve miles towards the Eden. By the ruins of Brougham Castle it is swelled by the River Lowther and meets the Eden at a point almost equidistant between Culgaith and Langwathby. This natural barrier divided Cumberland from Westmorland and, as I indicated in the opening chapter, was always something of a setback, particularly in winter months, for any traveller north.

Ullswater itself has been thoroughly described in other books and is rightly an important character in the chronicles of 'Lakeland'. I consider it to be beyond my brief, so I hastily turn towards Dacre Beck and the place and family to which it has given a name.

Dacre

Dacre Beck, a tributary of the River Eamont, has the distinction of being mentioned by St Bede in his *Ecclesiastical History of the English Peoples*, written in about 750. The name means 'the trickling stream', and there is a similar-named stream in the West Riding of Yorkshire. As in the case of the Yorkshire stream, the Cumberland one has given its name to a village, or, at least, to a place, and it is from the place that the warlike family of Dacre took its name.

The River Eamont separated Dacre parish from the neighbouring county of Westmorland on its southern boundary, while the other boundaries were shared with Greystoke, Penrith and Newton Reigny. Dacre is still a parish in its own right. In length it is about four miles from north to south, and $2\frac{1}{2}$ from east to west. The townships in the parish are Great Blencow, Newbiggin, Soulby and Stainton, besides that of Dacre itself.

Dacre 'town' is on the north bank of the Eamont. It is dominated by the tall keep of the castle, once the 'proud mansion of the Dacres, where the fierce old barons oft held high festival amidst their retainers, and where, protected by its ponderous walls, they could almost bid defiance to the majesty of the law'.

The family is going to need some understanding, and so I will begin gently. The Dacres came onto the scene of history when William de Dacre was appointed sheriff of Cumberland in 1249. Within three years he was also sheriff of Yorkshire and governor of both Pickering and Scarborough Castles. William's son, Ranulph, succeeded his father in both his sheriffdoms, and his son, another William, accompanied Edward I into Scotland. It was at about this time that he obtained a charter for 'free warren all his demesne lands at Dacre, and at Halton, in Lancashire'. On the sucession of Edward II Dacre was licensed to crenellate his mansion at Dunwalloght, in Cumberland, on the marches of Scotland. Three years later he was again engaged in the Scottish wars.

William's son, another Ranulph, was summoned to Parliament as Baron Dacre in 1321, and by marrying Margaret, the only daughter and heiress of Thomas de Multon, Baron Multon of Gilsland, he acquired considerable property, including Naworth Castle. Ranulph Dacre and Margaret Multon had three sons, each of whom was to succeed to the Dacre title in turn. Only Hugh, the youngest, who married Ela Maxwell, produced an heir, and this was William, the fifth Lord Dacre. William was summoned to the Parliament of 1384 and called as a witness in the celebrated heraldic case of *Scope versus Grosvenor* two years later. Married to Jane, daughter of James, Earl of Douglas, William was succeeded by his son Thomas in about 1403.

Thomas Dacre attended the Parliament of 1412. He was appointed Chief Forester of Inglewood by Henry V, and during the minority of Henry VI he was one of the commissioners to treat for peace with the Scottish king, James I. Thomas married Philippa Neville, the daughter of Ralph Neville, first Earl of Westmorland. Though there were several children of this union, of whom Thomas was the eldest, it was the fact of his death before that of his father that was to cause the barony to be divided in the following manner.

Thomas's marriage to Elizabeth, daughter of Richard Bowes, had given the couple a daughter, Joan, and Joan had married Sir Richard Fiennes, a rich landowner from the south, who was summoned to Parliament by Edward IV as Lord Dacre in right of his wife. The barony was to continue through the Fiennes family, so that they became known as 'the Dacres of the South', as opposed to the other branch, the descendants of Thomas Dacre's younger brothers, Ranulph and Humphrey, who became known as 'the Dacres of the North'. Ranulph, who was a strong supporter of the Lancastrian cause, was created Lord Dacre of Gillesland as a second creation, but in 1461 he was killed at the battle of Towton. He was subsequently attainted, and his title and estates became forfeit.

Humphrey was to fare better. He had 'deported himself obsequiously to the then triumphant House of York' and had attended Edward IV at the sieges and surrender of the different castles in the north. He shared his brother's disgrace but managed to survive the battle of Towton, and in time the attainder was reversed. Humphrey inherited his brother's title under a third creation, becoming Lord Dacre of Gillesland. He married Maud, a daughter of Sir Thomas Parr and aunt to Katherine, the future Queen of England, and he died in 1599, to be laid to rest at Lanercost Priory.

However interesting they turned out to be, we must not linger on the subject of 'the Dacres of the South' except to notice that the name Ranulph Fiennes came into the news a year or two ago, when, showing some of the nerve and energy of his illustrious ancestors, he marched across the North Polar ice cap. None will doubt where his courage originated: among the Dacres of the North!

Humphrey Dacre's son Thomas, second Lord Dacre of the third creation, fought at Flodden in the army of the second Duke of Norfolk; for his prowess he was made a Knight of the Garter. Dacre was in command of a body of horse reserve at Flodden but was engaged in several skirmishes with the Scots on other occasions as Warden of the West Marches, the office he had held since the beginning of Henry VIII's reign. Thomas Dacre's wife was Elizabeth Greystoke.

The Greystoke property eventually came into the possession of the Howard family, so that the barony of Dacre fell into abeyance. However, two members of the family tried to assume the title illegally, Leonard and Francis. The fate of Leonard Dacre is of some interest.

Leonard nursed a deep grudge that he had been dispossessed; his claim to the title had been disallowed. With little or nothing to lose, he decided to throw in his lot with the 'Northern Earls', the leaders of the 'Rising in the North', which was an attempt to dispossess Queen Elizabeth and place Mary, Queen of Scots, on the English throne. At the time the Scottish Queen was under house arrest at Tutbury Castle, in Staffordshire, to which she had been moved from Bolton.

We hear much these days about the north-south divide, but in Elizabethan times it was very much a reality and the folk of the north were considered almost a different tribe. England was something very separate from 'England beyond Trent'. For one thing communications were difficult, and the attitude of the people was that loyalty to their local lord took precedence over loyalty to the sovereign; Queen Elizabeth never travelled further north than East Anglia. The families that mattered were the Percies, the Nevilles, the Dacres and the Scropes (pronounced 'Scroop'). There was a remark of the time: 'They knew no prince but a Percy.' For the most part, in spite of the bitter reprisals after the Pilgrimage of Grace, the northern folk were still for the 'Old Religion' and had sensed a deep relief when England was received back into the fold of the Catholic Faith during the brief reign of Mary. For such feudal and religious allegiances, the possibility of deposing the 'bastard' Queen Elizabeth and replacing her by the Catholic Mary, Queen of Scots, was something to be desired and cogently worked towards. As Sir Ralph Sadler wrote in 1569, the year of the Rising, 'There be not, in all this country, ten gentlemen that do favour and allow of her Majesties procedings in the cause of religion.' The ancient faith lay like lees at the bottom of men's hearts; and if the vessel was ever so little stirred, came to the top.

The vessel was well stirred in the November of 1568. The focal point of northern religious life, Durham Cathedral, was seized and Mass was offered there, while anything smattering of Protestantism – communion tables and such like – was removed. In this part of the proceedings Leonard Dacre was not involved. What of him?

Dacre, instead of joining the rebels, set off for Windsor, where the Queen 'was contented, upon suit made by him, to admit him to her presence. When being privately with her, he made offers of his service against the Earls, being then proclaimed traitors; and most earnestly requested her majesty therein to commit trust to him, as to a most faithful subject and servant.' Dacre was sailing very close to the wind. He offered to join forces with the Queen's Warden of the Marches in service against the rebels. In fact all this time Dacre was corresponding with the rebels and 'encouraged them, promising great matters from the ambassadors of foreign princes; and, among other things, that he would cut off the Lord Scrope, Warden of the Western Marches, and the Bishop of Carlisle'.

After the rebel earls had fled into Scotland, Dacre saw his chance to seize some of the Dacre properties into his hands, including Greystoke Castle, and he fortified Naworth as his own inheritance. Under colour of defending his own and resisting the rebels, he 'gathered together three thousand of the rank-riders of the Borders, and some others which were most devoted to the name of the Dacres, which, in that tract, was a name of great reputation.'

Lord Scrope informed Cecil that there was little he could do in the circumstances: 'I dare assure you, that by the force of this country he is not to be touched; for that although I may levie a good number, yet very few will be found to execute their force against a Dacre.'

When the Earl of Northumberland's messenger was sent to Naworth to seek Dacre's immediate help, as the rebel forces were like to be utterly overthrown, Dacre desired the messenger to inform Northumberland that, as Scrope with all his power would be at Penrith on the following Tuesday, he hoped to attack him. 'If my company be great enough, I will set upon him, and overthrow him in the field, and if I think myself not able to meddle with his Lordship, I will return to my Lord of Northumberland with my whole power; and this shall be done, God willing, before Thursday night next ensuing.' He also indicated that he might be able to take Carlisle Castle. By the end of the next week Northumberland had heard nothing from Dacre; neither had he heard of any successes in the direction of Penrith or Carlisle. Dacre was, of course, playing a double game. By 24 December the Earl of Sussex was praising him for his great service in opposing the rebels. Dacre had stayed at Naworth. The rebel Earls had fled to Scotland when, in the following February, the Queen ordered Dacre's arrest. On 19 February Lord Scrope informed Cecil that 'Dacre has three thousand men, English and Scots; and all night the beacons burn.' The beacons were to call men to arms. Scrope issued a proclamation to the effect that, 'From hence, upon burning of any beacon, the people do make repair to none, saving only to the beacon of the Castle of Carlisle.' At the same time Sir Thomas Gargrave in York informed Cecil that he had heard by letter that 'Leonard Dacre had fortified Naworth Castle with men and munitions; and that he promised the aid of all the frontiers of Scotland, both of East, Middle and West.'

The battle was fought on 20 February. It was graphically described by Lord Hunsdon:

Yesternight, being the 19th of this instant, I took my journey from

> Hexham towards Naworth, at 9 in the night, and so marched all night; so as by day light I came before Naworth, the beacons burning all night; so as I found every hill full of men, both horsemen and footmen, crying and shouting, as though they were mad. And, understanding certainly that his house was full fraught both with ordnance, men and monycon, I determined to march to Carlisle, and there to join with my Lord Scrope; but Dacre's force was such, as he made full account of me and mine, and so sent me word, and offered me skirmish in sundry places; but I forbad utterly that no man should skirmish. And at last, when he had followed me four miles from his house, with these offers, in a heath, where we were to pass a river, his footmen gave the proudest charge upon my shot that ever I saw. Whereupon, having left Sir John Forster, with 500 horse for my back, I gave a charge with the rest of my horsemen upon his footmen; and slew between 3 and 400, and have taken 2 or 300 prisoners, such as they are. And Leonard Dacre, being with his horsemen, was the first man that flew, like a tall gentleman; and as I think never looked behind him, till he was in Liddesdale, and yet one of my company had him by the arm, and if he had not been rescued by certain Scots, whereof he had many, he had been taken. There were, by their own report, above 3,000 men, whereof above 1,000; and I was not, of all sorts, 1,500.

The following day Hunsdon informed Cecil that the pursuit of Dacre had gone three miles and that at one time he had been actually captured but had been rescued by the Scots. It was on this day that Dacre was proclaimed a traitor, for his 'divers and contemptuous and rebellious dealings'.

In his letter to Cecil Hunsdon he had not failed to think how he might personally benefit from the situation: 'I hope her Majesty will have some consideration for me, for so is her promise; and therefore, if it will please her Majesty to bestow Leonard Dacre's land upon mine own Yorkshire, I shall be better able to serve her.'

What Dacre had done was to cross the border into Scotland, from where he took ship to Flanders. In 1572 he was at Mechlin, in receipt of 100 florins each month from Philip of Spain and urging that monarch 'to be more assiduous in the task of freeing England'. A traitor indeed.

Dacre is thought to have died on 12 August 1573. He was

commemorated on a stone in St Nicholas's Church, Brussels, a church badly damaged in the Second World War.

Dacre Village and Church

It is always a joy for me to go into a church and see a really well-produced guide-book for sale; such was the case at Dacre, and anyone interested in this ancient and historic place should obtain *A Short History of Dacre Parish Church* by Philippa Smith. It was she who reminded me of Dorothy Wordsworth's reference to Dacre in her Journal for Friday, 9 July 1802: 'The trees are left scattered about as if intended to be like a park, and these are very interesting, standing as they do upon the sides of the steep hills that slope down to the Bed of the River, a little stony-bedded stream that spreads out to a considerable breadth at the village of Dacre.'

When I visited the church, dedicated to St Andrew, there was much activity going on in the churchyard, where archaeologists were 'digging' the site of the monastery mentioned by Bede as 'being built near the River Dacre'. It seems that the present church has been built on the site of this early monastic foundation. Although, as one would expect, the church was considerably restored in Victorian times, there are many features remaining of a church built in the late twelfth century, presumably replacing rather than involving any earlier church. The arcades date from the early thirteenth century, and the Norman tower, which was rebuilt in 1810, is an important and distinctive feature of the church.

Inside the church there are two ninth-century cross shafts finely carved and depicting scenes from the Old Testament. Outside at the four corners of the churchyard, are the Dacre bears. In 1704 on his visit to Dacre Bishop Nicolson noted: 'At each corner of the Churchyard, which is indifferently fenced, there stands a Bear and Ragged staff, cut in stone; which looks like some of the Achievements of the Honourable Family, which so long resided in the neighbouring Castle.' The Bishop was referring to the Dacre family, but the bear and ragged staff are part of the Warwick coat of arms. It has been suggested that the bears commemorate the marriage between Thomas de Dacre and

Philippa Neville, but their true origin is not known.

One further feature of the church is the lock on the south door, dated 1671 and marked with the initials AP. This is one of several locks presented by Lady Anne Clifford, Countess of Pembroke. These stock-locks were specially made by George Dent, of Appleby; each cost Lady Anne £1, and she gave them to anyone who had shown her particular kindness. There is a similar lock presented a year earlier to the Rector of Asby, near Appleby, which was a memento of the occasion when Lady Anne and her household were forced to take refuge from what she described as a 'mighty storm' on one of her journeys from Appleby to Pendragon Castle.

Dacre Castle

Like so many of the Cumberland castles, Dacre began as a single pele tower, but it has changed less than most other castles which have had considerable additions and alterations made through the years. Dacre was built in the middle of the fourteenth century. In 1354 Margaret de Dacre was granted a licence by Bishop Welton of Carlisle to have a chapel in the castle and for Robert de Kirkby to be her chaplain and confessor. In 1485 there was mention of 'a newly built tower' at Dacre. Although no details are known of the castle's use during the Civil War, by 1688 'Little remained of the castle but bare walls', and in 1695 a visitor noted: 'Here is a castle standing, which formerly has been a magnificent building and a seat of a family.'

In 1716 Dacre was sold to Sir Christopher Musgrave, and in 1739 S. and N. Buck issued a print showing the castle with saplings and grass growing out of the roof. In 1802 the moat was filled up and the outworks were destroyed; the principal parts standing were four square towers, composed of durable stone and connected by a central building. 'The windows are narrow and grated; the gloom which overspreads the interior is truly expressive of the dark ages of feudal tyranny.' Sir Christopher Musgrave had little or no interest in the casle and sold it to the Hasell family of Dalemain.

If we could be certain that it did happen here, the most important event to take place at Dacre was the meeting between

King Athelstan of England, King Constantine of Scotland and King Eugenius of Cumbria, in 926. The reference to this 'Peace of Dacre' occurs in the *Gesta Regum Anglorum* of William of Malmesbury, written early in the twelfth century. The event is unsatisfactorily explained beyond the fact that Athelstan received the homage of the other two kings; certainly not in what is known as 'the Room of the Three Kings' in the castle, because the castle did not exist at the time, but the meeting might have taken place at the monastery, for the pagan kings of Cumbria and Scotland received the sacrament of baptism.

Dacre parish comprised five townships, Dacre itself, Newbiggin, Great Blencow, Soulby and Stainton. Because of their positions north of the A66 and their close proximity to Greystoke, I shall speak of Great Blencow and Newbiggin in a later chapter, but Soulby and Stainton are very much part of the Eamont Valley.

Soulby, the 'village near the fork or joining of two rivers', takes its name from its closeness to the point where Dacre Beck meets the Eamont. The same name is found near Kirkby Stephen, where Scandal Beck meets the Eden. Soulby is a very small place situated on the south-eastern slopes of Soulby Fell, and very close to the Pooley Bridge and Ullswater. Stainton, 'the stone village', on the other hand, has seen considerable development in comparison owing to its closer proximity to Penrith. The same may be said of Tirril on the opposite side of the Eamont. However, by far the most important feature in the district lies between Soulby and Stainton: the large country house known as Dalemain.

Dalemain

The name appears early in the twelfth century, though the letter 'i' is missing, as might be expected, for Dalemain is 'Mani's dale or valley', where the Old norse '*dalr*' has become inverted, as in Dalegarth. The mansion is largely an eighteenth-century development of a building of the fifteenth century or possibly earlier. It is claimed that the oldest part of the house is a pele tower. I say 'claimed' because John F. Curwen makes no mention of it in his book on *Castles and Fortified Towers*, which suggests there is serious doubt. What is certain is the fact that the house has been in the possession of one family since 1680, when Sir Edward Hasell, the son of the rector of Middleton Cheney, in Northamptonshire, purchased Dalemain from the de Laytons. Edward Hasell had become secretary to Lady Anne Clifford, and after her death in 1675 he settled in Cumberland and married Jane Fetherstonhaugh of Kirkoswald. He was knighted by William III after he had sat as MP for Cumberland. Edward Hasell died seven years later, and Dalemain was inherited by his son, also called Edward, who was responsible for adding the fine east front to the house of nine bays with the middle five 'separated by rusticated quoins of even length'.

Dalemain (open to the public during the season) is furnished very beautifully and has fine portraits of the Hasell family and those connected with them. Of particular interest is the museum of the Westmorland and Cumberland Yeomanry Cavalry which was raised in 1819 by Edward Hasell, who was colonel for fifty years; for this alone Dalemain is worth a visit.

It is by Dalemain that the River Eamont takes the faster-running waters of Dacre Beck. It continues in its north-easterly direction, then suddenly swings round southward by Sockbridge Mill and rights itself as it passes Yanwath Hall. Now here there really is a fourteenth-century pele tower.

Thomas Machell, describing Yanwath, wrote: 'It hath a delicate prospect when you are at it, and hath the grace of a little castle when you depart from it.' This was in 1678; but the history of Yanwath, the 'even, level wood', began very much earlier than that. The name appears first in a record of about 1150 and is spelt 'Evenewit'. By 1200 it had been mentioned several times, 'Evenwith' and 'Yavenwith' appearing. I mention these because anyone seeing the modern spelling would almost automatically link the name with the Norse word for a ford, '*vath*', the position of the place being so close to the river, but the early forms show clearly that it is the Norse '*vith*', a wood, seen in Blawith Moss and Witherslack, that gave the name, tacked onto '*jafn*', which sounds very much like our modern 'even'.

The original pele tower was built in about 1322 by John de

Sutton, and the hall and kitchens were added some fifty years later by a member of the Threlkeld family. It was through the marriage of Grace Threlkeld to Thomas, Lord Dudley, in the 1520s that the hall came to be rebuilt and enlarged. It remained in the Dudley family's possession until in 1654 Christopher Dudley sold out to Sir John Lowther for a sum of £2,000, but it did not pass to Sir John until 1671, when, as he recorded, 'The Hall was left very ruinous.'

When Thomas Machell visited the Hall in 1679 he mentioned that he saw three coats of arms in the ceiling of the solar bearing the date 1586, when Edmund Dudley was in possession. There are also the royal arms over the mantelpiece in the tower.

Taken all in all, Yanwath was probably the best-looking house I have seen on my travels around the Penrith area. I felt rather as a visitor in 1811 felt: 'The Hall,' he said, stands on a precipice over the River Eamont. It is quadrangular; hath an agreeable aspect; and, at a distance, hath the appearance of a small castle. Over the gate hath been a chapel; and at the south corner has been a handsome tower, with turrets and battlements.' It was the chapel over the gate that caught my imagination.

Eamont Bridge

The bridge is '*on paere stowe pe genemned is aet Ea motum*', as they said in 1100, but there is the name. The passage reads in translation: 'on the place that is named at the river-confluences'. This refers to the meeting of the Lowther with the Eamont, '*aet Ea motum*'. It was by this bridge that a great Roman road, the High Street, crossed the river and continued north towards Carlisle, and until the motorway was opened Eamont Bridge was the last moment of Westmorland for the traveller.

The first mention of a bridge here is in 1300, and in 1362 John Marshall, vicar of Edenhall, left a shilling in his will for the maintenance of six bridges, of which Eamont was one. In 1380 there was a grant of pontage for six months for the 'repair of the bridges of Loutherbrig and Amotbrig'. The money was to be taken from merchandise passing over or under the bridges or 'by the Castlewath of Burgham' – that is, the ford by Brougham Castle.

In 1425 the first stone bridge was built. Thomas Langley, Bishop of Durham, made a grant of forty days' indulgence to any who should contribute adequately towards the building of a new stone bridge across the waters of Amot. The Bishop was also Lord Chancellor, Cardinal and Papal Legate. Not for nothing are bishops sometimes called '*pontifex*' – 'bridge-builder'.

The later records concerning the bridge are less romantic, but there are full accounts of work intended in 1871 and 1874, and in 1926 HM Office of Works informed the County Council that the bridge was 'a monument the preservation of which is of national importance'. The Society for the Protection of Ancient Buildings wrote at the same time insisting 'that this noble medieval structure should be maintained. In its way the structure is comparable to the other great structural feats of the Middle Ages – though not on so large a scale as the cathedrals of England, nor even as the magnificent oak barns, it is representative of medieval civilization and thought as any building of either of these classes.' In future we shall have to drive over this noble pontifice more reverently.

From Eamont Bridge the Eamont and the Lowther run more or less parallel with each other until they meet by Brougham Castle. On the way they pass on the north side Carleton Hall with its tall radio mast, the headquarters of the Cumbria Constabulary. Carleton, 'the farm of the free men or peasants', was a separate manor and gave its name to a family which held it until 1707, at the death of Robert Carleton. It was then sold to John Pattinson and through successive daughters passed to the Simpsons and the Wallaces. The Right Honourable Thomas Wallace sold Carleton in 1828 to John Cowper. Carleton Hall is, like Penrith town hall, 'Adamish', with a good-looking Georgian front.

Brougham

Brougham is an extensive parish lying between the Rivers Eden, Eamont and Lowther. In the rural deanery of Penrith but part of a united benefice with Clifton and Cliburn today, Brougham has an illustrious past, chiefly through its having been an important Roman station and its fine castle being linked with the name of Lady Anne Clifford.

To the Romans Brougham was Brocavum, situated on the banks of the River Eamont at the point where it meets the Lowther about 250 yards south-east of the castle. The fort immediately south-east of the castle, with the longer axis running north-east to south-east, was 120 yards by 180 yards, in all taking up an area of $4\frac{1}{2}$ acres, if one accepts that the Roman north ditch became the southern part of the castle moat. Archaeological evidence would suggest that Brougham was a military cohort-fort, but there have been no traces of internal buildings discovered. Fragments of pottery from the second to the fourth centuries were found when the south moat of the castle was cleared, and a hoard of coins was unearthed about a hundred yards from the north-east side of the fort in 1910. The coins dated from the time of the Emperor Vespasian to that of the Tetrici.

Whatever importance the Roman fort might have had is surely surpassed by that of the castle, the stronghold the Normans built close by and which later generations were to improve. The castle is built largely of sandstone, the red sandstone of the district. It is associated with the Clifford family and remained in their possession until their descendant Lord Hothfield placed the castle under the guardianship of the Office of Works in 1928. Today the castle is in the good hands of the Department of the Environment. The keep of the castle is the earliest part; this was built towards the end of Henry II's reign, at some time between 1170 and 1180; known later as 'the Pagan Tower', it is still impressive to anyone approaching Penrith along the A66. At first this was the only part of the castle built in stone, the outer buildings having been wooden with a main courtyard surrounded by a strong stockade and ditch. Originally it was two storeys high, but a third floor was added at the end of the thirteenth century by Robert Clifford at the same time as he built the outer gatehouse and chapel. Little of the original chapel survives, but a later two-storeyed chapel block built by Roger, the fifth Lord Clifford, may be seen on the west side of the courtyard.

The manor was first granted to de Meschines but passed to the Vipont family late in the twelfth century when King John granted it, as part of the confiscated estates of Hugh de Morville, one of Becket's murderers, to Robert de Veteripont. The King made the proviso that Veteripont or his men should not 'commit waste in the woods of Whinfell' or hunt there during the King's lifetime in the absence of Robert de Veteripont.

Isabella de Veteripont married Roger, Lord Clifford, and brought the castle with her as part of her dowry. There is an inscription to Roger, the fifth Lord Clifford, set into the wall of the outer gatehouse above the entrance. It was Roger Clifford's grandson, Robert, who built much of the castle.

In 1403 the castle was attacked by the Scots, and the building and lands were considered worthless 'because it lieth together waste by reason of the destruction of the country by the Scots'. Some years before, the King of Scotland himself had been a guest at the castle. In the winter of 1333-4 King Edward Balliol had been entertained by Robert de Clifford, a visit to which a well-known legend is associated. When Clifford took the King hunting in Whinfell Forest, the pair chased a stag with a single greyhound out of the forest and as far as Redkirk in Scotland and back again. The distance is almost certainly an exaggeration but there is no reason to doubt the fate of the two animals: 'Both being spent, the stag leapt over the pales and died there: but the greyhound, attempting to follow, fell and died on the opposite side.' The horns of the stag were nailed to a tree, where they remained until the end of the seventeenth century. The hound's name was Hercules, and it is remembered in this couplet:

Hercules killed Hart-a-grease,
And Hart-a-grease killed Hercules.

It should perhaps be explained that 'grease' here is the French '*graisse*', meaning fat, and implies that the stag was a well-fed beast.

In the Wars of the Roses the Cliffords fought for the Lancastrian party. John Clifford inherited the estates after his father was killed at the first battle of St Albans, so called, though it was hardly a battle in the conventional sense, a skirmish, rather. Clifford became known as the dreaded 'Blackfaced Clifford'. At the battle of Wakefield he brutally murdered the young Earl of Rutland, brother of the future Edward IV, for no greater reason than that he was of the House of York. Not only this ruthless murder but, as an eye-witness account gives: 'Not content with this homicide or child-killing, cruel Clifford came to the place where the corpse of the Duke of York lay, caused his head to be stricken off, and set on it a crown of paper, and so fixed it on a pole, and, presenting it to Queen Margaret saying "Madam, your war is done; here is your king's ransom:" at which present was much joy and great rejoicing, but many laughed then that soon lamented after.'

Only three months later, at the battle of Towton, John Clifford was killed when an arrow pierced his throat. The Clifford estates were seized by the Crown, and the Clifford heirs were forced into hiding. The younger boy was sent over to Flanders but, according to legend, Lady Clifford placed the elder, then only seven years old, in the care of a shepherd on the estate at Londesborough, in Yorkshire, who brought him up as his own son. Lady Clifford later married Sir Lancelot Threlkeld, who was instrumental in saving the life of young Henry Clifford, 'the Shepherd Lord', as he came to be called. Later, when Henry VII came to the throne after the battle of Bosworth, all the Clifford estates were restored to Henry and, as Wordsworth put it:

> Glad were the vales, and every cottage hearth;
> The shepherd lord was honoured more and more;
> And ages after he was laid in earth,
> 'The good Lord Clifford' was the name he bore.

However, no member of the Clifford family bore a better name than Lady Anne Clifford, who lived in the seventeenth century and is best remembered for the loving care with which she restored several Westmorland castles, including Brougham.

Lady Anne was the only daughter of George Clifford, the third Earl of Cumberland. She was born at Skipton Castle in Craven in 1590. Her mother was Margaret Russell, who had been betrothed to George Clifford when they were both children, in the presence of Queen Elizabeth.

Lady Anne can have barely known her father during her childhood; he was an Elizabethan adventurer, often abroad. On eleven occasions he fitted out a fleet in order to plunder foreign ports or intercept merchant ships from the Spanish or Portuguese trading centres. Lady Anne seems to have inherited her father's sense of determination.

She was to be married twice: first to Lord Buckhurst, who became Earl of Dorset, when he was nineteen. This marriage lasted for sixteen years and took her to Knole, in Kent where she spent much of her time. The marriage was not a happy one, though Anne remained loyal throughout. Six years after Dorset's death, she married the Earl of Pembroke and Montgomery, an equally unhappy alliance. She had borne Dorset five children, two of whom survived, but had none by her second marriage, as she was now forty. By the marriages of her two daughters she became grandmother to eighteen children. Her daughter Margaret having married John, Lord Tufton, in 1629 to become the Earl of Thanet, the Tuftons came to inherit the Clifford estates after Lady Anne's death in 1675.

The Clifford castles and land had been one of the constant interests and, indeed, worries of Lady Anne's life. Much of her time during her marriage to Dorset had been spent in a state of anxiety over her rightful inheritance, for her father had left all to his brother and his heirs in his attempt to keep the estates in the family. Those interested in the details of Lady Anne's life should read Martin Holmes's excellent biography *Proud Northern Lady*. But all that needs to be said now is that Lady Anne eventually did come into her estate in 1643, when she was fifty-three years old. It was then that she set about restoring her castles and many local churches: rebuilding St Michael's Bongate in Appleby, and St Lawrence's there also, besides Ninekirk, near Brougham Castle. She owned six castles: Skipton, Barden, Pendragon, Brough, Appleby and Brougham, the first two in Yorkshire, the remaining four in Westmorland. She spent some time at each, making certain that the buildings were in good repair and adding, altering and improving where her whim took her. At Brougham she removed the old bakery buildings and erected others as part of a vast programme of repair and rebuilding. There is stone commemorating her work in one of the outer gatehouses at Brougham, no doubt placed there by herself, and with a quotation from the Prophet Isaiah: 'And they that shall be of thee shall build the old waste places: thou shalt raise up the foundations of many generations; and thou shalt be called, The repairer of the breach, The restorer of paths to dwell in.'

On the south side of the A66 about a mile from the castle may be seen the Countess' Pillar, erected by Lady Anne in 1656 to mark the spot where she said goodbye to her mother for the last time forty years earlier.

The two churches at Brougham either restored or built by Lady Anne are St Ninian's, known as Ninekirk, and St Wilfrid's. In fact, although there had been an early church on the site at Ninekirk, what may be seen today is a complete rebuilding carried out in 1660. It is situated a little over a mile from the castle on the north-east side, above the Eamont.

St Wilfrid's Chapel, to the south-west of the castle, was built under Lady Anne's guidance in 1658. The fact that fourteenth-century masons' marks and consecration crosses have been found on several of the stones led some to think there had been an earlier church on the site, but there is no tradition of this. The chapel was considerably altered in the 1840s by Lord Brougham, and for many years it was best known for its magnificent Flemish triptych that was eventually considered too rare and valuable to remain there. It was restored by the Victoria and Albert Museum and may now be seen beautifully displayed in Carlisle Cathedral.

Brougham Hall

The great house built between the years 1830 and 1840 was the home of the famous Lord Chancellor Henry Brougham, Lord Brougham and Vaux, but it was demolished in 1934, so that all that remains to be seen is part of the stable block. In its heyday Brougham Hall was known as 'the Windsor of the North', and it was constructed on the site of the earlier home of the family, the de Burghams.

In the time of King John Brougham was granted by Robert de Veteripont to Gilbert de Burgham, and the manor remained with that family until by marriage it passed to John de Vaux of Catterlen and Tryermayne. In 1676 James Bird, a steward of

Lady Anne's, purchased the estate, and so for three generations it was 'alienated' from the Broughams, who later bought it back for £5,000. In 1756 Henry Brougham, the grandfather of the future Lord Chancellor, inherited the estate. This branch of the family had lived at Scales, in Cumberland, but the exact link with the ancient de Burghams is not known.

Henry Peter Brougham was born in Edinburgh on 19 September 1778. He was the eldest son of Henry Brougham and his wife Eleanor Syme, and the house of his birth was at the corner of the West Bow and Cowgate. In later life Henry Brougham claimed to be a descendant of the de Brougham family of Brougham Castle and from the barons of Vaulx, both titles he was to claim when he raised to the peerage in 1830, but it seems that this was wishful thinking on his part. He was, in fact, descended from the Broughams of Scales Hall in Cumberland, a member of which family, Peter Brougham, had bought a parcel of land in the parish of Brougham on which Brougham Hall was later built. Henry Brougham's father inherited the hall with its land.

Educated at the Edinburgh High School, whence he was sent at the age of seven, Henry Brougham became Head Boy and left there in 1791. For a year he lived in Westmorland and continued his studies at Brougham Hall under a tutor. In October 1792 he returned to Edinburgh to take up a place at the university. A brilliant undergraduate, Brougham delighted in the study of mathematics and physics, and when only eighteen years old he published a paper on 'Experiments and Observations on Light'. While at the university he became revered as a debater, and after the four-year course in humanity and philosophy he moved over to study law.

In 1800 he began to practise at the bar and later, through the influence of Lord Holland, Brougham entered Parliament for the first time as member for Camelford in 1810, making his maiden speech on 5 March that year. Within four months he was taking a major part in most debates for the Opposition, and he moved an address to the Crown on the subject of slavery.

Brougham's father died in 1810 and from then onwards he made Brougham Hall his chief home when he was not in London.

It was probably as early as this time that he began to claim a direct connection with the ancient de Brougham and Vaux families, for which there is no evidence whatsoever.

In the House of Commons Brougham 'did good service both in drawing attention to the importance of popular education and devising means for its attainment'. Obtaining reappointment to the education committee in 1818, he instituted an inquiry into charity abuses, which he extended to the universities, Eton and Winchester, much to the resentment of the governing bodies when the inquisition revealed scandalous irregularities. In June 1820 Brougham brought in two bills providing for 'the compulsory building, the government, and the maintenance of parochial schools'. His proposals were disliked by the Dissenters and fell through.

In this same year came the royal divorce, the most famous occasion when Brougham appeared as an advocate. His magnificent performance in the Queen Caroline trial made his reputation even greater, and in 1828 he made a speech on the 'present state of the law', which lasted for six hours. In 1830 he was appointed Lord Chancellor under the administration of Lord Grey, and in this important position he was able to do much to lay down new procedures and to establish new rules for the Court of Chancery, besides simplifying High Court procedure. He also set up a new court to hear bankruptcy cases, which is ironic since it was the bankruptcy of the fourth Lord Brougham that would lead to the estate's being sold in 1931.

There was, however, an even greater irony in the fact that Brougham had been appointed to such high office only because his colleagues were afraid of him in any other. Nevertheless, in spite of major embarrassments (such as his tour of Scotland in 1834, described as a 'vagrant, grotesque apocalypse', and his turning up at a race meeting paralytically drunk, wearing his Lord Chancellor's robes, perhaps creating a precedent for the Lord Chancellor of W.S. Gilbert), Brougham did play a major part in bringing in the Great Reform Bill of 1832.

In 1835 he was excluded from Lord Melbourne's ministry, and when he demanded a reason, he was told: 'You domineered too much, you interfered too much with other departments, you encroached upon the provinces of the Prime Minister, you worked, as I believe, with the press in a manner unbecoming to the dignity of your station, and you formed political views of your own, and pursued them by means which were unfair towards your colleagues.'

Brougham was not to hold office again, but he continued to play an active part in the House of Lords, having taken the title of Lord Brougham and Vaux, both familiar names. He died at Cannes at the age of eighty-nine, in 1868, an example of what Grenville called 'a very remarkable instance of the inefficacy of the most splendid talents'.

In 1804 Sidney Smith had said of Brougham: 'He impresses me more and more with a notion of his talents and acquisitions.' It is with Sidney Smith that this chapter will end. He was once travelling by coach from Edinburgh, to visit Brougham, when he fell into conversation with two Scottish girls. When they heard where he was bound, one of the girls said to him: 'Why, you must be a very remarkable man to be going to Brougham Hall.' 'I am a very remarkable man, ma'am.' The girls left the coach at Penrith, and Sidney Smith travelled on another mile or so to visit his friend, an equally remarkable man, as his colleagues named him: 'Old Wickedshifts'.

7

The Leith Valley

'I am come home.'
Charles Edward Stuart, 1745

The River Leith rises in Shap parish and flows parallel with the Lowther, though separated from it by the hills of In Scar and Out Scar, which form a watershed for both rivers. It is from the scars that the Leith takes its name, the Old English '*hlith*', meaning a slope or hillside providing its base. The Leith's course is not very long, some ten miles only, before it meets the Lyvennet at a point about a mile east of Cliburn, and after flowing more or less due north from its source to Meklinthorpe, it swings due east for the rest of its journey. The Leith influences several attractive villages not often seen unless sought out in the land between the two important main roads, the A6 and A66, ever narrowing. Good grazing land this, as the name of the first place indicates, which is Strickland or 'Stirk land', the land on which young cattle are pastured.

Great and Little Strickland

Both Great and Little Strickland were formerly townships of Morland Parish, but in 1870 Great Strickland was united with nearby Thrimby to form one parish. Today, it is part of the united benefice of Morland, Great Strickland, Thrimby. However,

Strickland was always one manor, and the 'Great' and 'Little' served only to distinguish the two parts of the holding. The family that was to take its name from the manor became one of the most illustrious in Westmorland through the marriage of Sir William Strickland and Elizabeth Deincourt in 1239. Henry II had granted the Deincourts Sizergh, near Kendal, besides estates in Lincolnshire, and Sir William was fortunate in his marriage, but the Stricklands had become important in their own right before this time. Henry III gave permission for the family to have a private chapel at their Great Strickland home, and the Bishop of Carlisle agreed to it, provided it did not 'injure the revenues of the mother church of Morland'. Sometime between 1231 and 1236 Sir Walter de Stirkeland received permission from the abbot of St Mary's at York to have a chantry for the private use of his family in the chapel attached to his house at Strickland. Again the rights and revenues of the mother church at Morland were retained; the chaplain was to be subservient to the vicar, and Sir Walter undertook that he and his entire household would attend the parish church on the four great feast days of the year.

After being in the possession of the Strickland family for some two hundred years, Strickland passed during the reign of Henry VI to the Fallowfields. It is not known whether this was by 'marriage, purchase or grant', but it was by a marriage that the manor was conveyed to John Dalston of Acorn Bank, Temple Sowerby, and it was a Christopher Dalston who eventually sold the manor to Sir John Lowther, so that it now forms part of the Lowther Estate.

The school at Great Strickland was founded in 1790 and the schoolhouse rebuilt in 1848, the cost being wholly defrayed by Sarah Plumer, the wife of the Reverend Charles Plumer of Elstree, in Hertfordshire. This great act of charity was for the benefit of 'poor persons in the township of Great Strickland and neighbourhood' and provided that the master or mistress should be a member of the Church of England and competent to teach. The school at Great Strickland is nothing like as old as the one founded for Little Strickland and Thrimby, in 1684. In that year Thomas Fletcher made provision for a curate and schoolmaster 'to perform divine service in Thrimby Chapel and teach English and Grammar there'. Until 1834 the two duties were performed by one man, but in that year it was decided that the two offices should be held by distinct persons, each of whom should receive £5 a year from Thomas Fletcher's original endowment of £10.

Little Strickland is a small hamlet with a group of farms. The school is now closed, and I found the small church locked. It is dedicated to St Mary and was built in 1814. There are several very attractive seventeenth- and eighteenth-century houses, of which the best are Low Hall, an L-shaped building of about 1600, and High Hall, which is probably about the same age.

Great and Little Strickland are about two miles apart, Little Strickland being south of the larger village, but this is not as far south as Shap, nor as the two places I shall speak of next.

Reagill and Sleagill

Although Reagill, 'the ravine haunted by foxes', is in Crosby Ravensworth parish, which is really outside the Penrith area, for the purposes of this book I include it because it was situated a little too far north of the area I covered in my book on the Howgills, and because one name has made the place interesting, for Reagill was the home of Thomas Bland, an extraordinary man who painted and composed music but chiefly occupied his time in sculpting strange shapes and figures which may be seen in the garden of his home.

Thomas Bland was the son of a local farmer and was born in 1799. He was completely self-taught and an example of what is known as a 'primitive'. Nothing is known of his artistic ventures before the celebrations marking the accession of Queen Victoria in 1837, when he opened his garden to the public for the first time. From then on this became an annual event on the anniversary of the first occasion. In 1860 a festival of a somewhat unique character is described: 'Mr Bland's garden is richly ornamented with pictures, and statuary. A band of music is engaged for the occasion, and the day's amusements are interspersed with lectures, addresses, music, dancing, and other recreations.' On one such occasion Anthony Whitehead, the Reagill poet, 'appeared as a giant, walking on stilts, covered over with robes, wearing a flowing beard and carrying a huge staff, and recited a poem of his own composition relative to the feats of the character he was representing'.

Bland's more public sculptures were the monument to Queen Victoria at Shap Wells and a smaller monument at Black Dub, where the River Lyvennet rises, to mark the occasion when Charles II rested with his troops on 8 August 1651 on his way to the ill-fated battle of Worcester.

It is said that David Cox, the younger, wished to introduce Bland to a wider public, but he refused. He died at Reagill in 1865.

It was fortunate for Thomas Bland that his brother William was a farmer and could keep him in supplies, but he must have made some income from his annual festival, when as many as fourteen hundred are said to have attended.

Sleagill

Sleagill, 'the trickling stream', is with Kings Meaburn, Newby and the Stricklands one of the townships of Morland parish. From early records it seems Sleagill was linked with Newby, and in the reign of Edward II, for instance, it was described as 'Sleagill, in the hamlet of Newby'. Anyway, the manor was included in that of Newby and like it was part of the barony of Kendal. It was originally held by a family bearing the name of the place, who passed it to the Staffolds. In Charles I's reign William Fayrer is named as holding some property in Sleagill, as did the Blenkinsops. In 1670 William Mawson sought the consent of the dean and chapter of Carlisle to lease the tithes of Sleagill to the vicar of Penrith, but when the commons were enclosed in 1803, the tithes were commuted for an allotment of land.

Sleagill is situated in a small valley where a narrow beck hurries northward toward Newby and Morland and eventually meets the River Lyvennet by Crossrigg Hall, near Cliburn. I imagine the stream is known locally as Sleagill Beck, but it is soon adopted by Newby and becomes Newby Beck. (Unlike the rivers, the small becks, and even smaller 'sikes', tend to take their names from the nearest hamlet or village, so that the instance I have just mentioned is common where what is really one stream changes name as it moves forward to join something

Mardale flooded – Haweswater

Swindale from Rossgill

The Eamont at Brougham

(*overleaf*) Dufton and Dufton Pike

Askham

The Steamer sails – late afternoon, Ullswater

The castle at Greystoke

An East Fellside farm

St Laurence's – Morland

The sawmill at King's Meaburn

larger.) The road from Sleagill to Newby Head, which is the west end of village, takes a more direct route than the beck but gives us a good view of the region.

Newby

One of the townships of Morland Parish, Newby – or, as it was once called, Newby Stones – is situated about a mile and half from Morland. In a record of about 1160 it appears at 'Neubi', and the name means simply 'the new farmstead'. It was in the sixteenth century that the form 'Newby upon Staynes' was first seen, for which there has been no satisfactory reason given. A map published in 1777 would indicate that Newby village was given this name, and the Early English Place-Name Society suggests that the allusion could be to several old limestone quarries to the west of the village on Stone Hills. The sites of these old quarries may be clearly seen along the narrow road to Lansmere.

The early history of Newby is vague beyond the fact that it was a manor held by a family that took its name from the place. In the reign of Henry VIII part of the manor was granted by the King to Richard Vernon, sixteen messuages or dwelling places, and three hundred acres of land. The family that came to Newby next, the Nevinsons, continued to hold it for many generations, and it was they who built and occupied the Hall before, like so much else, it became Lowther property.

Although the Nevinsons are first recorded as living at Newby in 1556, they do not seem to have started work on the Hall until the early seventeenth century. The building is H-shaped with two storeys and attics and has been recently ruined by being divided into four self-contained flats, a temporary measure, one hopes. Above the main doorway is a late seventeenth-century achievement-of-arms of Nevinson set in a square panel, and the simple forecourt, though in need of attention, makes Newby Hall one of the most attractive small manor houses in Westmorland.

Morland

The village of Morland is a delightful little place which has grown up where Newby Beck, now reinforced by Greengill and Copeland Sykes, flows on to join the Lyvennet.

Morland, 'the wood on the moor or marsh', appears in a record of 1133 as 'Morlund', where the Old Norse '*lundr*' meaning a small wood or sometimes a sacred grove is more obviously seen with the Old English '*mor*'. The strange part about Morland's history is that it was part of the ancient barony of Kendal while being situated fairly obviously in the region of the Appleby or Westmorland barony. It was thus never owned by either the Veteriponts or the Cliffords but was granted by William de Lancaster to Alexander de Windesore sometime between 1160 and 1170, together with the manors of Grayrigg and Heversham and the hand of his daughter Agnes in marriage. It was one of Alexander de Windesore's descendants, William de Windesore, who obtained the grant to hold a weekly market and an annual fair in Morland in 1362.

Ecclesiastically, Morland is interesting, having the only Anglo-Saxon tower in Westmorland or Cumberland at the west end of St Laurence's Church. The church was granted by the barons of Kendal to St Mary's, York. Sometime between the years 1092 and 1125, Ketel, Baron of Kendal, confirmed the grant that had formerly been made by Ivo de Tailbois. Later, when Hugh, Bishop of Carlisle, confirmed the grant on 20 October 1220, he stipulated that the church was for the use of the monks of Wetheral and for the support of the poor and of strangers.

Something of how highly Morland was regarded is seen by the value put on the church in the thirteenth century. It was the custom for the pope to allow taxes that might ordinarily go to Rome to be collected by the king if the latter had expenses incurred in any campaign that might be considered to be fighting for the Church's cause. The most obvious example of this was the part the king took in the Crusades. In 1291 a tax known as the *Antique Taxatio Ecclesiastica* was granted by Pope Nicholas IV to Edward III for a period of six years, toward defraying the expense of an expedition to the Holy Land. In the list of benefices and their values, Morland is valued at the high figure of £80 and the vicarage at £26.13s.4d. This tax, although high, might have been acceptable in time of peace, but the levy had been made just before the long war for Scottish independence, and that wasteful and debilitating struggle made it quite impossible for the parishes to keep up their payments. The situation was understood at Rome, and Pope Clement V ordered the collectors in the devastated areas to the south of the Border to ascertain once more the 'true value' and to tax accordingly. The *Novo Taxatio* was levied in 1318 by virtue of a royal mandate that Edward II directed to the Bishop of Carlisle. The value of Morland went down to a more realistic figure: £13.6s.8d. for the church and £4 for the vicarage, figures that remained more or less constant until the reign of Henry VIII, when the parish was granted to the dean and chapter of Carlisle.

Visitors to Morland will welcome the excellent guide to the church written by the Reverend Canon Gervase Markham to commemorate the 800th anniversary of the church in 1979, The guide contains three photographs showing how the church looked before its restoration in 1896. The photograph of the church's exterior gives a very good idea of how many parish churches looked as the eighteenth and early nineteenth centuries had left them before the Victorians took upon themselves necessary, but often too radical, reconstructions: the tower and much of the nave and chancel covered with ivy and what appear to be saplings growing out of the roof. Canon Markham describes in great detail the various stages of the church's development. It is interesting to note that Edward I visited Morland on 4 October 1292 and spent the night there, and as it was a Saturday he would almost certainly have attended Mass in St Laurence's the following morning. The King had been travelling north, and he made this stop between Appleby and Brougham, where he spent the Sunday night.

In 1699 it was recorded that there was a school held in the south transept of the church and that John Thompson was the master. The school had been founded some fifty years earlier. On 31 March 1653, during the Commonwealth, the Commissioners for propagating the Gospel in the four northern counties of Northumberland, Cumberland, Westmorland and Durham directed that, 'Whereas there is exceeding great need for a school at Morland in the county of Westmorland it is ordered that the tithes of Scattergate and Burrels of the yearly value of £20, late of the Dean and Chapter's lands be granted to and for the maintenance of a school master at Morland and being satisfied of the ability and due qualification of Thomas Todd for that employment, we do hereby constitute and appoint the said Mr Todd master of the school.'

Thomas Todd was succeeded by John Pears, second master and parish clerk, who died on 18 January 1664. Neither of these two, however, seems to have been remembered in the way John Thompson was to be. Thompson moved from Morland to Barton, where he died in 1736, a man 'of the most exemplary piety, probity and sobriety. A great admirer of and well versed in the pliter sort of literature.' His pupils, one suspects, will have been unware of the escapes of Moll Flanders and Clarissa Harlow.

In 1780 the inhabitants of Morland by their subscriptions and labour built a proper schoolhouse, which, like the mill, is now part of the premises of Survival Aids Ltd, a remarkable piece of private enterprise which supplies equipment to soldiers, climbers and field sportsmen and organizes courses at their Survival Training Centre, instructing in shelter-building, fire-lighting, cooking, water-purification, day and night navigation, first aid and much else besides.

Someone who might well have been glad to have learnt the rudiments of survival was William Wilson of Morland, who on 15 October 1821 was sentenced to transportation beyond the seas 'as the Privy Council shall direct for a period of seven years. His crime was stealing a coat, a waistcoat, two silk neckcloths, a cotton pocket handkerchief and a pair of leather gloves, all items that might well have been tantalizingly presented to him in the Survival Aids catalogue!

King's Meaburn and the Lyvennet

The River Lyvennet rises in a small pool, Black Dub, where, it may be remembered, Thomas Bland had placed a monument to Charles II; then, racing down Crosby Gill, a good nutting area, as the name Hazel Moor indicates, it flows more or less due north through Crosby Ravensworth and Mauld's Meaburn until it reaches King's Meaburn, which is some two miles, as the crow flies, south-south-west of Morland.

The name of the river probably means 'the smooth sliding' or 'slippery one', but its exact stem is uncertain. It has been suggested that the name may be that of one of the settlements situated in the parish which has survived as a river-name, which seems most unlikely.

More is known about the manor of Meaburn, 'the pasture stream', which is divided into two and forms two separate villages. The reason is that the manor was one of the holdings of Hugh de Morville, who had to forfeit his estate soon after the murder of St Thomas at Canterbury in which he took a leading part. It is not certain if this was directly owing to the murder or to a later difficulty de Morville had with Henry II.

The northern part of the manor became Crown property, as the name King's Meaburn suggests, but the southern part was settled upon Hugh's sister Maud, who could not have been guilty of her brother's impetuosity. The spelling of Maud's name at the time is seen in various forms, but often it was something like 'Mahald' or 'Mald', and so the place became 'Mauld's Meaburn'. Maud de Morville married William de Vipont, which is an added reason for such an advantageous settlement in her favour. I have seen it stated that the division took place earlier and that the father of the two children, Roger de Morville, had settled the manor on them, but this is not the accepted view on the evidence.

King's Meaburn is four miles or so north of Mauld's Meaburn and has for long been a township of Morland parish; its long 'street' has many attractive houses, a good inn, the Bay Horse, and an interesting part of the Lyvennet, for at King's Meaburn it flows through a deep gill, Jackdaw Scar, cut into the sandstone. The Lyvennet then continues northwards to meet the River Leith near Cliburn.

Cliburn

The name means 'the stream by the bank'. In 1250, or thereabouts, a record of Wetheral Priory spells the name 'Clyfburne', where the 'clif' which also appears in 'Clifton' is clearly shown, although the earliest record spells the name 'Clibbrun'. The cliff presumably refers to one of the scars beside the River Leith, or possibly to the small hill on which the village itself stands. It has been suggested that the Cliburn hill may be the '*hlith*' which gave the river its name.

Cliburn is situated some two miles north of Morland and three miles south-west of Temple Sowerby. Many will know the village by its inn, the Golden Pheasant, a good place to draw off the hasty A66 in all weathers. The main street runs north to south with attractive houses on either side downhill towards St Cuthbert's Church and the large farm of Cliburn Hall, both looking down upon the river as it flows eastwards with only four miles to go before it is gulped up by the greater Eden.

The Hall was originally the home of the family that took their name from the place. In the fourteenth century Robert de Cliburne built a fine pele tower to which his descendant Richard de Cliburne added to in 1567. The date is given on a tablet above the front door, and if one modernizes the inscription, there is a neat couplet:

> Richard Cliburn thus they me call
> Which in my tyme hath builded this hall.

The manor of Cliburn is revealing in its history, for it shows that for many years it was divided into two moieties, Cliburn Talbois and Cliburn Hervey. Perhaps I should explain: a 'moiety' is a 'mediety' and literally meant splitting something into two halves, though it sometimes came to mean a portion of a manor. There are also examples of the word being used by a man for his wife in the sense of his 'better half'.

The two moieties of Clifton took their names from the Tailbois family, who were barons of Kendal, and the Hervey family, of whom there is no record apart from the name. The Tailbois family continued to hold their part of the manor until the tenth year of Henry V's reign, 1422. Eventually both parts of the manor were united and passed to the Cliburne family. During the reign of Richard II, Richard de Cliburn was Knight of the Shire for Westmorland. As with so many manors in the region, Cliburn was later mortgaged to the Lowthers, and it is now owned by the Earl of Lonsdale. In fact, the Cliburns and the Lowthers intermarried, Thomas Cliburn married Frances, daughter of Sir Richard Lowther, who was Warden of the West Marches, but only for one year, 1592, on the death of Henry, ninth Lord Scrope, before

Thomas, the tenth Lord, took over in 1593 and remained in office until the abolition of this old title on the accession of the King of Scotland to the English throne in 1603.

The little church dedicated to St Cuthbert stands back from the village street and is approached by a short avenue of lime trees, five trees on either side, leading to the steps and wrought-iron gate into the churchyard. The church is largely a reconstruction put up in 1886 on the site of an earlier building, but much of the masonry of the nave and chancel is Norman. Of particular interest are some fragments of stone in the porch inscribed in Roman times and found during the restoration.

As in the case of Morland, Cliburn was appropriated to St Mary's Abbey at York. When the first Bishop of Carlisle, Athelwold, confirmed the appropriation, it was 'with the stipulation that the said abbot should allow a decent maintenance to the officiating minister'.

Among the miscellaneous items that appear in the early records of Cliburn are one or two worth noting. In the Assize Roll for 1256 we read: 'Emma daughter of William de Cliburn appealed against Adam de Eunethweyt for the death of Adam her husband killed in her arms. So that by her suit he is outlawed in the county; his chattels are not known because he is a stranger from the county of Cumberland. And because the jurors are informed that the aforesaid Adam was killed in the village of Cliburn and the same village did not arrest Adam therefore it is in mercy.' During Michaelmass 1379 Robert de Cliburn sent his attorney, Adam Crosseby, to appear on his behalf against John de Stirkland of Melkinthorpe, who with Thomas Williamson had cut down and carried away the trees and underwood belonging to Robert de Cliburn, and with certain beasts they trod down and consumed his 'corn and herbage lately growing there'.

Such records give us fascinating glimpses into the past; some are complicated legal wrangles, while others are short and to the point, as is that of 2 January 1706: 'Thomas Cowper of Cliburn yeoman, was indicted for keeping a greyhound not being qualified so to do.'

While the plague raged at Appleby in 1598 it was to Cliburn, a distance of seven miles, that the Appleby folk came to market.

This was at Gilshauglin, west of the village, a place with an apt name, as it happens, since it means the 'gill or ravine of the infirm walkers'.

Bolton

Before moving north-westward towards Penrith again, it is important to notice Bolton, one of the townships of Morland but which, because of its closeness to the main road, the A66, seems to be associated with the villages to the east of it, Long Marton and Crackenthorpe, and the town of Appleby.

'Bolton' is 'the enclosure with the buildings' or 'the village proper' and is common to several North Cumberland place-names. The earliest record spells the name 'Botelton', but the Holme Cultram Register's reference to 'Bothelton' shows the Old English '*boþl*', 'a dwelling', more clearly.

In 1314 the manor of Bolton was held by Ralph de Greystoke, but it passed subsequently several times to different families until it was purchased by the Lowthers. In 1326 there was an inquisition held at Appleby as to who ought to furnish the chantry in the chapel of Bolton, and a survey of 1649 lists the chapel as belonging to Morland, but with 'one house for the curate abutting upon the churchyard'. Some years later, in 1657, it was recorded that, 'There is a parochial chapel at Bolton two miles south-east distant from the parish church of Morland which hath no maintenance belonging to it only the vicar of Morland is to find a Reader there and hath usually paid him yearly £7 out of his tithes and glebe lands.' The readers or curates at Bolton are listed until 1829, when Edward Jackson was at Bolton. He must have been familiar with one of Bolton's treasures. On the north side of the fabric built into the wall over the window are two sculptured stones which appear to date back to the time of Henry II. There is still an effigy of a lady in a praying position, 'weathered and framed by ivy', outside the church.

Bolton church is dedicated to All Saints, and there are, besides the praying lady, several interesting Norman features, particularly a relief of two fighting knights on horseback above the north door. However, most of what may be seen is of the restoration carried out in 1848.

South of the village, some two miles away, are the ruins of Bewley Castle, situated on the banks of Sweetmilk Sike, a tributary of the Eden. The castle was erected in about 1170 and was originally known as 'Fithnenin', but it became known as 'Beaulieu' in the thirteenth century through rather strange circumstances, for that name is usually associated with the Montagu home in Hampshire, which was formerly a Cistercian abbey.

The castle at Fithnenin, 'the river-side pasture', was granted by Ucthred de Botelton in about 1170 to the church at Carlisle. After the death of Bernard, the second bishop, in 1186, the diocese remained vacant for thirty-two years, during which time the canons appointed their own bishop and swore fealty to the King of Scots. This situation naturally annoyed Henry III, who applied to Pope Honorius III, who gave orders for the canons to be expelled, and Hugh, Abbot of Beaulieu in the New Forest, was appointed Bishop of Carlisle in 1218. The following year the castle was allotted to the new bishop, who gave it the name of his mother-house. The name 'Beaulieu' is a French form of the Latin '*bellus locus*', 'beautiful place', and it appears in its Latin form in several Westmorland documents.

It is known that Bishop Silvester used Beaulieu, or Bewley, as a residence, since two deeds were executed by him from there. In about 1325 there were considerable alterations made to the building, and Bishop Strickland restored the castle, particularly renovating the chapel and the solar.

Melkinthorpe

The name means 'Melkan's hamlet', but nobody can tell who the particular Melkin was, although attempts have been made to identify him with the Melkin of a medieval romance about the battle of Stainmore.

Melkinthorpe is not a place one passes through, not nowadays anyway, since it is a cul-de-sac, but in earlier days the fords across the River Leither led one to Melkinthorpe Hall and a road that linked the place more directly with Great Strickland along the south bank of the river. However, like so many of the smaller places, Melkinthorpe was in earlier times a manor in its own right.

Beginning as part of the marquis fee of the barony of Kendal, it was later held by a family that took the place's name, so that a Galfrid de Melkinthorpe was Constable of Appleby Castle under Roger, Lord Clifford. Not that Appleby Castle was unfamiliar to the folk of Melkinthorpe, for in 1257 unknown 'malefactors broke into the house of Geoffrey de Melinthorpe and Richolda his wife, cut their throats and carried away their goods'. The entry in the Assize Roll continues: 'Afterwards Warin de Melkinthorpe, Adusa Frikes, and Agnes de Breweress were taken for the same burglary and imprisoned in the castle of Appleby, from which prison the said Warin escaped in the time of Ralph de Nottingham, then Sheriff.' Warin seems to have made a successful get-away, but Adusa was hanged and Agnes 'delivered in the presence of the Justices'.

Melkinthorpe Hall was, in fact, in Great Strickland, but it was the home of the de Melkinthorpe family until it passed to the Musgraves and afterwards to the Fallowfield family, whose heiress transferred it by marriage to the Dalstons, who sold it to the Lowthers. Once described as a 'little, low, mean-looking building', the Hall was rebuilt in the sixteenth century, and it was demolished some time during the nineteenth. All that remains of the outbuildings is a barn lit by two ranges of loop-lights. Today, Melkinthorpe has one or two well-kept houses with names such as 'Fossils' and 'Rose Cotage', but there is no church, no inn and no old hall – in fact, no focus. The folk seem contented enough.

Clifton

Two miles north-west of Melkinthorpe is the last village I shall look at in this chapter, Clifton, which is well known to all who travel towards Penrith on the A6, and to the historian, because of the battle that took place there on 18 December 1745.

Clifton, 'the farmstead on the cliff', is so called, according to Nicolson and Burn, 'from two very remarkable cliffs above which it stands'; these cliffs overlook the River Lowther close to the point where the railway line crosses over it.

The village has grown up along the A6, and it was, of course, very much busier in the days before the M6 motorway was built which passes it by on the western side. The positioning of the motorway has meant that Clifton is cut off from its oldest monument, a cromlech of two megalithic stones set about nine feet apart, the larger of which is six by three feet compared with the four by about 2½ feet of the smaller.

Another important 'monument' at Clifton is the well-known Wetheriggs Country Pottery associated with the Schofield family. When the Brougham estate was sold up in 1932, the Scholfields, who had worked the pottery since the 1860s, were able to purchase the buildings together with the local inn, the George and Dragon. Today the pottery carries on the traditions of English slipware and is well worth a visit.

It is known that the Romans occupied the Clifton area because when the railway was under construction the navvies unearthed a Roman altar, on the sides of which were the figures of a vase and *praefericulum* with a Latin inscription showing that the altar was dedicated to Jove.

In the reign of Henry II the manor of Clifton was granted by Sir Hugh de Morville to Gilbert Engayne, whose descendants continued to possess it till the year 1364, when Eleanor, the heiress of the family, brought it in marriage to the Wyberghs of St Bees.

Clifton Hall was largely pulled down in 1800, and only the original pele tower remains. In 1819 Joseph Robinson noted that the Hall was reduced to a solitary tower and that its slated roof and sash windows spoilt 'that interest which we should otherwise feel in contemplating the ancient edifice'.

The tower had been built in 1364 and rebuilt to make it stronger in 1475. On 17 December 1745 it was occupied by the Jacobites and plundered by them, which was ironic in a way since Thomas Wybergh of Clifton Hall had suffered heavily for his Royalist sympathies in 1652 and was in the list of delinquents whose estates were ordered to be sold. It was noble to support the Stuarts, but the right ones and at the right time.

The part Clifton played in the Jacobite Rebellion of 1745 is well described, as we shall see, by Lord George Murray who led the rearguard of artillery, but as the two rebellions of 1715 and 1745 were to involve the people of the Penrith area as a whole, it is important to know something of their background.

Penrith and the Jacobite Rebellions

The first Jacobite Rebellion, in 1715, had very little effect on the Penrith area, although there was quite a bit to see as the rebel supporters marched south towards Preston. However, there was considerable support in the north for the Old Pretender, James Stuart, as the Government had been aware, having taken the precaution of detaining several of the local leaders and imprisoning them in Carlisle Castle. Among these were Howards, Warwicks and Curwens, but the leading members of the Dacre family of Lanercost were laid low with a fever.

The Highland supporters of James (he who was considered by his supporters to be James VIII of Scotland and James III of England and, no doubt, would have been so had it not been for his adherence to the Roman Catholic Faith) had arrived at Longtown on 30 October 1715 and advanced as far as Brampton, careful to avoid the fortress at Carlisle where there would be opposition. At Brampton they were joined by the Earl of Derwentwater and 'a parcel of North-country jockeys and foxhunters'. The rebels marched out of Brampton towards Penrith, which they reached on 2 November and where they received a contribution of £500. The only opposition they were to meet in the area came from the Westmorland Militia, an odd assortment of folk, as may be seen from this contemporary newspaper account:

> They appeared with their pitchforks on the very ground through which the rebels were to march, and most of their parsons were with them, applauding their zeal and courage. This unanimity and good understanding between the priests and people continued till about one o'clock, when no enemy appearing abroad, and great gnawings being felt within, and not opportunity of refreshment in view, the infantry began to drop off, and continued to do so until (about three in the afternoon) we had advise that the rebels were coming towards us. I cannot say that this raised our spirits. They were so much sunk and our enemies knew it. In short they marched on, and we marched off. The very sheriff though a gentleman of good personal courage and undoubted loyalty, was beaten down with the universal deluge of despair; and Lord Lonsdale had not twenty besides his own servants, who continued with him till the triumphant Lord Derwentwater,

> Lord Nithsdale and company appeared in sight; and then in imitation of the great example of a very good lord we wisely retreated.

From Penrith the Jacobites travelled by way of Appleby, Kendal and Lancaster to Preston, the cavalry entering that town on 9 November and the infantry the following day. The rebel army was disorganized and weakly led, and it failed to hold Preston; on 14 November the whole force was disarmed. Seventy-five English and 143 Scottish gentlemen and nobles and a little over a thousand rebel Scots and English were captured. The Lancashire recruits who had no uniforms were able to disperse unnoticed. The rebellion anyway was not a formidable one and had little hope of success from the start. The Earl of Derwentwater was later executed for high treason and his lands were confiscated.

The second Jacobite Rebellion, thirty years later, in 1745, made a far deeper impression on the area than the '15, and it is true to say that had the first rebellion been as well led as the second the whole history of the country might well have been very different. In 1715 the followers of the Stuarts had been numerous; by 1745 they were fewer, and Prince Charles was misled as to what support he might expect.

The Prince landed on the small island of Eriskay on 23 July. The story is well known of how he was at first received coldly, and when one of the chieftains advised him to return home, he replied 'I am come home.' Soon support began to gather and at Prestonpans the Jacobites won a crushing victory, after they had taken Edinburgh. When the news of Prestonpans reached Carlisle, the city was speedily prepared for defence, and seven hundred militiamen from Cumberland and Westmorland were drafted into the city. Despite these preparations under Colonel Durand, Carlisle capitulated to the rebels on 15 November. The following day James III was proclaimed at Carlisle Cross, the mayor and corporation attending the ceremony in state. At Brampton the next day Charles received the keys of the city, and on the 18th, riding on a white charger and accompanied by a hundred pipers, he entered the city. The road to the south now seemed open to him.

In fact, on the very same day billeting officers arrived in

Penrith; their requirements were accommodation for two squadrons of cavalry, who would arrive the same night, and for eight thousand infantry, who would reach the town the following day. The officers had over-estimated the numbers involved, but it was best to be on the safe side; nevertheless, it must have been something of a relief for the townsfolk. Early in the morning of 20 November arrived the Duke of Perth, Lord George Murray, who was the Prince's Commander in Chief, Lord Elcho and a chieftain with the splendid name of Gordon of Glenbucket. The next day the Young Pretender himself entered the town. He was clad in full Highland dress and rode before a regiment of foot. His quarters were to be at 19 Devonshire Street, where today there is a plaque to record the fact.

While they were at Penrith, stores were brought in from the neighbouring large estates. A thousand stone of hay was needed for the cavalry, and ten cartloads of oats. Dalemain, Eden Hall, Hutton John, Hutton Hall and Greystoke Castle all complied, but Lowther Hall refused, with the result that the place was occupied by a hundred horsemen and, after the troops had left, the Hall was plundered.

It is said that the townspeople were treated with courtesy by the rebels, who were particularly popular with women, although there was little courtesy in the treatment of Richard Skelter, a tallow chandler, who was carrying a 'potato pot' from the bakehouse when a burly clansman accosted him and grabbed the dish from his hands.

How the clansmen fared after leaving the town is not the business of this book to relate, as it is well known that Prince Charles's intention of marching on to London was frustrated at Derby when he was overruled by his generals.

The retreat from Derby was a disordered affair and became even more so when the rebels arrived in Westmorland. They reached Kendal on 15 December, a market day, and were mobbed by the crowd; several people were killed as a result. The claim that the Prince and the pursuing Duke of Cumberland slept in the same bed on consecutive nights in a house in Stricklandgate seems a little far fetched, though it could be true.

Westmorland weather made the going very difficult as the

retreating soldiers crossed over Shap. In the attempt to reach Penrith from Kendal in one day, the rain and wind made it impossible to go further than Shap, and many of the artillery failed to get even that far, some ammunition waggons having broken down.

The details of this part of the retreat were graphically recorded by the Chevalier de Johnstone who, with three companies of the Duke of Perth's regiment, had been detailed to escort the artillery, reinforced by five hundred men from the Macdonalds of Glengarry. 'We set out from Shap at break of day, on the 18th, to join our army, which waited for us at Penrith; but we had scarcely begun our march, when we saw a great number of the enemy's light horse continually hovering about us; without, however, coming within musket-shot.' The Chevalier goes on to describe how at first they had thought there was a large contingent of the English army in the vicinity because of 'a prodigious number of trumpets and kettle-drums' that could be heard, when the Highlanders attacked, however, 'We were agreeably surprised when we reached the top of the hill to find, instead of the English army only three hundred light horse and chasseurs, who immediately fled in disorder, and of whom we were only able to come up with one man, who had been thrown from his horse, and whom we wished to make prisoner to obtain some intelligence from him; but it was impossible to save him from the fury of the Highlanders, who cut him to pieces in an instant.'

The events that took place at Clifton were reported by Lord George Murray. When the Highlanders drew near to Clifton on the afternoon of the 18th, the Duke of Cumberland, with his dragoons, was close upon them.

> I now observed small platoons of horse appearing on eminences at some distance behind me, of this I sent word to the prince, but, at Penrith, they had taken a notion that it was only militia. There was indeed a body of 200 or 300 light horse, being, I believe, mostly Cumberland people, that drew up in my way, thinking to obstruct our march; but as soon as the Glengarry man threw their plaids and ran forward to attack them, they made off at the top gallop, and gave me no more trouble. When I came to Clifton, I sent off the cannon and other carriages to Penrith, being two miles further; and as I

believed these light horse that had met me would probably be near Lord Lonsdale's house at Lowther, as he was lord-lieutenant of the county, I went a short way with the Glengarry men to that place through several enclosures, it being not above a mile. Lord Pitsligoe's horse had joined me, so I was in hopes, by scouring these enclosures, to meet with the light horse. We got sight of several hard by Lord Londale's house, but could come up with few; at a turn of one of the parks one like a militia officer, clothed in green, and a footman of the Duke of Cumberland, were taken. We understood by them that the Duke with a body of 4,000 horse, as they said, were about a mile behind. I sent Colonel Roy Stewart with the prisoners to Penrith, and to know his royal highness' orders, and that I would stop at Clifton, which was a good post, till I heard from him. When I came back to Clifton, the Duke of Perth was there; and besides Colonel Roy Stewart's men, being about 200 that I left there, Cluny with his men, and Ardshiel with the Appin men, were with them. The Duke of Perth, who was there, had been persuaded that it was only militia that had appeared; but he then saw, upon an open muir not above cannon shot from us, the enemy appear and draw up in two lines, in different divisions and squadrons. His grace said he would immediately ride back, and see to get out the rest of our army; for as the ground was strong where I drew up, he did not doubt I could maintain that post till others joined me. I sent an English gentleman with him who had attended me all the retreat, and knew the country perfectly well, who said he would lead them a near way by the left, undiscovered, that they could fall on the enemy in flank; and as there was a lane that lay betwixt Lord Lonsdale's enclosures, which was near a mile in length, and through which the enemy had come, if they were obliged to retire they would suffer much by both sides of the lane if we lined it. I only desired 1,000 more men than what I had, by which means I could not only maintain the post I had, but send half of my men through the enclosures on my right, so as to flank the enemy on that side, if they were attacked on the other side; and if once but twenty of their horse could be killed, it would make such an embarrass in the lane, that it would put them all into confusion, and choke up the only road they had to retreat, except the Appleby Road, and that also might be secured, which would give us an advantage that, perhaps, we should not meet the like again.

Lord George Murray describes considerable action during the night:

> The moon, which was in its second quarter, from time to time broke out and gave good light; but this did not continue above two minutes at a time.
>
> We advanced, and had a good deal of fire on both sides. After the Highlanders on that side had given most of their fire, they close at an open hedge, which was the second in these fields. We then received the whole fire of the dragoons that were at the bottom, upon which Cluny said: 'What the Devil is this?'. Indeed the bullets were going thick enough. I told him we had nothing for it but going down upon them sword in hand, before they had time to charge again. I immediately drew my sword and cried 'Claymore.' Cluny did the same; and we ran down to the bottom ditch, clearing the diagonal hedges as we went. They were a good many of the enemy killed at the bottom ditch, and the rest took to their heels, but received the fire of the Glengarry regiment.

After this there was no more firing and Lord George Murray ordered the retreat.

> It was lucky I made the stand at Clifton, for otherwise the enemy would have been at our heels, and come straight to Penrith; where after refreshing two or three hours, they might have come up with us before we got to Carlisle. I am persuaded that night and next morning, when the van entered Carlisle, there was above eight miles from our van to our rear, and mostly an open country full of commons.

In the Clifton parish register of burials there is the following entry: 'The 19th day of December, 1745, the dragoons, to wit, six of Blands, three of Cobham's, and one of Mark Kerr's regiment, who were killed the evening before by the rebels in the skirmish between the Duke of Cumberland's army and them at the end of Clifton Moor.' After such losses it is hardly surprising that fierce reprisals were taken against the Highlanders after they were defeated at Culloden.

8

The Barony of Greystoke

'I am so much with my sick friend ... I have not time to spare.'
William Wordsworth, November 1794

There is something grand and well ordered about Greystoke – I should, perhaps, say 'noble'. Part of this nobility lies in the way the name must be pronounced: there is more of the stock-broker about it than stoker, which should make the matter clear. Those who have the chance to see early records containing the name would have no difficulty. The first recorded spelling is 'Creistoc'; that was in 1167. 'Creistok' appears in 1359, and the name begins with either a C, K or G in many other records. The most probable explanation of the name is derived from the spelling 'Crekestock' which was used in 1171. Here the '*creic*' may be the Old Welsh name for a hill and would presumably refer to the high ground to the north-west of the village; and the '*stoc*' element is the Old English for 'place'. It is worth noting that the *Oxford Dictionary of English Place-Names* suggests that the first element may be a river-name, 'comparable with the name of the river Cray in Kent, and refers to the stream which joins the Petteril to the north of Blencow'.

Greystoke gave its name to a barony which embraced all that part of Cumberland lying between Inglewood Forest and Ullswater on the north and south, and the seigniory of Penrith and the manor of Castlerigg, near Keswick, on the east and west. Greystoke came into existence during the reign of Henry I, who had retaken possession of Carlisle and formed the two counties of Cumberland and Westmorland. Cumberland (which already consisted of three baronies, Gilsland, Lyddale, or Liddell, and Burgh-by Sands, established by Ranulph de Meschines) was further strengthened by the creation of five more baronies, Copeland, Allerdale, Wigton, Greystoke and Levington, while the Crown continued to reserve the city of Carlisle and Inglewood Forest.

Within the limits of the Greystoke barony were the parishes of Greystoke and Dacre and part of Crosthwaite. Today, as we have seen, Dacre is still a single parish, while Greystoke, with Matterdale and Mungrisedale, forms a team ministry, though we may still speak of Greystoke parish from the 'civil' point of view.

Henry II confirmed the grant of the Greystoke barony to Phorne, the son of Lyulph, properly spelt 'Ligulf', the modern form having been popularized when in the eighteenth century the Duke of Norfolk built and named Lyulph's Tower on the north side of Ullswater. Phorne was the first to adopt the name of the place and became known as Phorne de Greystoke. The barony was held of the Crown *in capite*, which means that it was a direct grant from the king in return for 'serving the king in person against Scotland' and the payment of £4 annually to be paid at Carlisle at the time of the fair.

The direct descendants of Lyulph and Phorne held Greystoke until the time of Henry III. Thomas de Greystoke, the seventh Baron, had been made a ward of Robert de Veteripont when his father, William de Greystoke, died, and when he came of age he married de Veteripont's daughter Christian. It was to Thomas that Henry III granted the right to hold a weekly market on a Saturday and an annual three-day fair to commence on the Eve of the Translation of St Edward. Two of Thomas de Greystoke's sons were to inherit the title, and his daughter Joan, who married William fitz Ralph, Lord of Grimesthorpe in Lincolnshire, was the mother of the Ralph fitz William, who eventually inherited the title when his cousin John de Greystoke, the tenth Baron, died childless in 1306.

Ralph fitz William served Edward I at the siege of Calaverock and was rewarded with the governorship of Berwick on Tweed and the wardenship of the Marches, which he shared with Lord Mowbray and others. Edward II appointed fitz William Governor of Carlisle, a position he held until he died in 1317. It was Ralph fitz William's grandson, another Ralph, who assumed the name of de Greystoke, so that the name continued for another five generations. When Ralph inherited the title, the land was described as worth 'by the year in all issues at this time £621 13s. 9d. and no more, because it is destroyed by the Scots'.

The Grimesthorpe family remained in the title until it passed through the female line when Elizabeth de Greystoke inherited as a child in 1506. Elizabeth was to marry Thomas, Baron Dacre of Gilsland, and by this marriage the two baronies were united.

The wolf-dog and bull supporters of the Dacre's three escalloped arms seemed to bring energy to the family. The son of Thomas Dacre, William, was appointed Governor to Carlisle and Warden of the Western Marches by Edward VI, in 1549. In one or the other of these offices he remained during the following reigns. It was not until towards the end of Queen Elizabeth's reign that Greystoke was to fall into the happy hands of the Howards, the family that had seen several of its members rise to sudden fame, only to be struck down on the scaffold.

Through the untimely death of George Dacre on 17 May 1569, his three sisters, Anne, Mary and Elizabeth, were appointed co-heiresses. All three were wards of the Duke of Norfolk, who proceeded to marry them off to his three sons. Anne married the Duke's eldest son, Philip, Earl of Arundel, who died in the Tower in 1595 for his Catholic faith and is now St Philip Howard. Mary married Thomas Howard of Walden, first Earl of Suffolk, the son of the Duke's second wife, Margaret, daughter and sole heir of Thomas, Lord Audley of Walden, in Essex, and Chancellor of England. Elizabeth Dacre married Lord William Howard, the Duke's second son by his second wife. Greystoke has remained in the Howard family ever since.

As the husband of the eldest of the three sisters, it was Philip who became Baron of Greystoke. He was Earl of Arundel through his mother, Mary, the daughter of Henry Fitzalan.

Greystoke Castle

There has been a house of some importance here since very early times, and it was reasonably suggested by Lady Mabel Howard in 1923 that the 'first House commences when Lyulph was owner of Greystoke'.

Ivo, son of Phorne, is thought to have built the manor house of Greystoke. This was the building whose large central tower with the three dungeons is still part of the castle. In 1353 William de Greystoke obtained permission to castellate from Edward III. He is thought to have built three towers, one of which is incorporated into the present building, the other two being destroyed during the Civil War.

William de Greystoke was a considerable benefactor to the 'town', and it was he who founded the college. Nicknamed 'Le Bon Baron', he obtained episcopal and royal licence to establish a college in place of the previous rectory, the college to have a master and six chaplains. However, William died before the scheme could be completed. He was buried in the church; it is possible that one of the effigies in the church represents him.

Very little is known about the early history of the castle. In 1570 it was forfeited to the Crown when the rebel Leonard Dacre fled to Scotland after 'the Rising of the North'. There is a record dated 1580 which states: 'This house or castle doth belong to the heir of the late Leonard Dacre standing about eight miles east and by south from Cockermouth Castle and about eighteen miles from Scotland, and yet for sundry good considerations meet to be repaired, the charge whereof with help of the woods there belonging to the lord and owner of the same.' It was thought at the time that the moat could wait 'till a greater necessity.'

In the summer of 1648 the castle was largely destroyed by fire by order of Major Chomley, who led a detachment of General Lambert's troops: 'The quadrangular building with four towers was destroyed'. The result was that beyond a few fragments nothing of the medieval building remained. In about 1675 Henry Charles Howard rebuilt the castle. In 1789 it was enlarged and considerably altered by Charles, the eleventh Duke of Norfolk. 'Greystoke Castle is a large, old building,' wrote James Clarke in his *Survey of the Lakes*. 'It is only two stories high, but the Duke is preparing to raise it a third.' Later, under the direction of Anthony Salvin FSA, Henry Howard restored the castle to its present form. When, in the May of 1868, another fire occurred internally, Salvin returned to Greystoke, and his 'ambitious and correct neo-Elizabethan mansion' still impresses when the sun lights up the pink stone.

Greystoke College

The foundation of the college, as I have said, was owing to the beneficence of William, fourteenth Lord of Greystoke. The upgrading of Greystoke from a rectory was thought necessary, possibly because the rector seems to have been non-resident. During the incumbency of Ralph de Ergholme, who was rector from 1314 to 1357, the church buildings were in a sorry state of repair. His successor, Richard de Hutton Roof, anxious about the state of things, 'took out a commission of enquiry into the state of the buildings in 1357'. It is thought that this prompted William, Lord of Greystoke, to found the college, though building does not seem to have begun very swiftly. When later in the century the Bishop of Carlisle carried out a visitation, Greystoke church was found to be still in a state of dilapidation, 'its walls ruinous, the belfry collapsed and the roof largely open to the sky'. The Bishop ordered immediate repairs on pain of excommunication.

Action was taken and the college was reconstituted to have eight priests instead of six. A certain Gilbert Bowet was appointed master. The priests of the college were 'chantry priests' whose chief work was to offer Masses for the souls of the faithful departed and in particular for their founder and benefactors. Greystoke church contained six chantry chapels; these were dedicated to Our Lady, St Andrew, to whom the church itself was dedicated, St John the Baptist, St Thomas of Canterbury, St Katherine and St Peter. The dissolution of the college probably occurred in 1549, during the reign of Edward VI, but the exact date is unknown. From that time Greystoke returned to being a rectory.

Little remains of the medieval church apart from the thirteenth-century arch and one or two minor features, such as the fifteenth-century fireplace in the priest's chamber. Most of what may be seen today is a nineteenth-century rebuilding of the church restored in 1645 during the incumbency of William Morland, who, with Thomas Howard, Earl of Arundel and Surrey, paying for the work, made the church what it is. These were indeed difficult times to be building, and Morland was deprived of his living during the Commonwealth on the grounds of 'ignorance and insufficiency', but he was reinstated when Charles II was restored to the throne.

Perhaps the main feature of the church is its height; as the little guidebook says, it is 'of noble proportions outwardly and refreshingly spacious within'. The stubby-looking west tower was wholly rebuilt in 1848, but nevertheless it has kept its medieval proportions.

As Arthur Mee once said, 'Greystoke stands out among its simple neighbours like a gem.' The attractive houses round the green, the impressive castle gates, give a general feeling of well-being. For my part, I prefer some of the less illustrious Cumbrian villages, Dufton or Great Salkeld, for example. There is something almost 'southern' about Greystoke.

In 1958 Greystoke became once more a 'collegiate town', for a scheme was started, as at Brasted, in Kent, to assist young men who felt they had a vocation to the priesthood and yet lacked the academic qualifications to enter a theological college immediately. The students lodged in the village, attended lectures and, of course, used the church, saying or singing the Offices in much the same way as the original priests of the ancient college. The rector of Greystoke was also the warden of college, and there was a chaplain-tutor. This situation continued until the college closed in the 1970s.

One of the stewards of the Duke of Norfolk at the castle was called Calvert, whose son Raisley became famous not so much for his painting and sculpture, in which he dabbled, but because of his close friendship with William Wordsworth, to whom he left a legacy of £900 in his will.

Raisley Calvert was born in 1773 and was, as Wordsworth said, a 'worthy short-lived youth', since he died in 1795 at the age of twenty-two.

Calvert had an elder brother, William, who had been a

contemporary of Wordsworth at Hawkshead and was the friend who accompanied the poet on a tour of the west of England during the summer of 1793, which ended disastrously when the 'whiskey' in which they were travelling was involved in some kind of accident. Calvert deserted his friend and, as Dorothy Wordsworth reported, 'mounted his horse and rode into the North'.

On the death of Raisley Calvert senior in 1791, William inherited property at Ormathwaite and Crosthwaite, near Keswick, while young Raisley received a sum of money of which the Duke of Norfolk was trustee; it was part of this that eventually came to Wordsworth.

During his last days, Raisley was nursed by Wordsworth at a house in Penrith after a proposed trip to the more salubrious air of Lisbon had failed to materialize. There is a plaque on the outside of the Robin Hood Inn in the town to commemorate the fact. In November 1794 Wordsworth wrote to a friend: 'I am so much with my sick friend ... I have not time to spare.' Raisley Calvert died early in January 1795 and was buried in Greystoke churchyard. Later in life Wordsworth seemed to belittle his friendship with Raisley and spoke of 'but little connection' with him. The legacy, he said, was given 'entirely from the confidence on his part that I had powers and attainments which might be of use to mankind'. Humility was never one of Wordsworth's strong points, to put it kindly.

Another Greystoke name that became well known through death is that of Isabel Foster, who was born in the village but moved to London and became the wife of a cutler living in Fleet Street. Together with six others Isabel was burnt at the stake at Smithfield for her Protestant faith during the reign of Queen Mary.

To the east of the village along the B5288 are situated three late eighteenth-century farm buildings, all of them follies and the whim of the eleventh Duke of Norfolk. The two on the south side of the road, Fort Putnam and Bunkers Hill, are strange castle-like buildings, while Spire and House, as its name suggests, has a polygonal tower with a recessed spire; all have the 'Vanbrughian ring of the tower of Greystoke Castle'.

The River Petteril

It is on the slightly higher ground to the west of Greystoke village that the River Petteril rises. A tributary of the Eden, the Petteril flows in a north-easterly direction for a while towards Great and Little Blencow; then, at a point about half a mile past Laithes, it is met by the waters of the Old Petteril and flows on towards Newton Reigny, its most southerly point before its long stretch northward again towards the Eden.

At Blencow the river provided a useful boundary, so that Great Blencow was always in Dacre parish and Little Blencow in Greystoke. The family that took its name from the place has an illustrious past. Adam de Blencow distinguished himself during the Hundred Years' War and was granted arms for his service by William, Baron of Greystoke. In 1617 Henry Blencow was knighted – by King James I, on his return from Scotland. He was High Sheriff of Cumberland, a post he continued to hold until his death in 1635. Sir Henry was married twice, first to Jane Musgrave, whose sister Eleanor was married to Sir James Lowther, and secondly to Grace Sandford.

The family home, Blencow Hall, is situated a little south-west of the village along the Greystoke road. It bears the date 1590 over the door, though some of the building seems earlier, a simple hall range between two low towers. It seems likely that the north tower is the earlier of the two; the date 1475 is assigned to it by John. F. Curwen. The south tower is thought to be early sixteenth century. The buildings occupy two sides of a courtyard entered by an arched gateway on the south-west.

The small hamlet of Laithes is first mentioned in a record dated 1292. In 1575 it is referred to as 'Blencoe-Lathes'. The name is derived from the Old Norse '*hlaths*' meaning a barn. There is a Helsington Laithes near Kendal, and the same element is seen in Laithwaite and Colby Lathes. No doubt there were store places here in early times. Today there is a goodly farm, and at one time there was a mill situated at the eastern end of the 'town'.

Great Blencow, as I have said, was part of Dacre parish. The village was once more important than it is today and had a well-endowed grammar school which was founded in 1577 by

Thomas Burbeck, a native of the village. Burbeck had endowed the school, which at first taught nothing but classics, with land in Northamptonshire besides land nearer home at Culgaith. In 1793 it was rebuilt and a master's house added. In 1884 Thomas Fawcett, a Bachelor of Arts from Queen's College, Oxford, was headmaster and had 'accommodation in his house for boarders'. Among the eminent pupils of Blencow Grammar School was George Whitehead, the famous Quaker, who had been born in 1636 at Orton, in Westmorland.

Another pupil of Blencow was John Huddleston, the priest who shelterd Charles II after his defeat at Worcester and who reconciled the dying King to the Catholic Church on 1685.

About half a mile south of the village there is a house named Ennim Bank, said to have been the original home of the Blencow family during the reign of Edward III before they moved to the Hall. In the middle years of the last century Ennim was described as the 'pleasant seat of George Troutbeck Esq., who has greatly improved the mansion and ornamented it with plantations'. The name is interesting, being the Middle English '*innam*', meaning a piece of land, taken in or enclosed.

Catterlen

Catterlen is situated almost due east of Blencow, close to the M6. The first time the name appears, in 1158, it is written 'Kaderleng'; then in 1165 it is spelt 'Caderlen', which looks as though the Old Welsh '*cateir*', meaning a chair, is here used for a mountain, as in Cader Idris in Merionethshire. If this is so, it might refer to one of the two hills west of Catterlen. An alternative suggestion was put forward at the beginning of this century by a Dr Taylor, who drew upon two Hiberno-Celtic words, '*ceather*', 'the quadrangle', and '*leana*', 'of the river-side marsh'. Possibly '*cateir*' and '*leana*' have come together.

What is certain is that Henry II granted the manor to Hubert de Vallibus, the name that was later to become Vaulx or Vaux. Several generations of the Vaux family held Catterlen before William de Vaux died in 1481. It is thought to have been he who built the pele tower still to be seen at the Hall. This is almost certainly the second tower, for, as John F. Curwen notes, there was some kind of fortification erected by John Vaux in 1170.

Catterlen Hall today shows three stages of building: the pele tower, an Elizabethan wing to the north, built in 1577, and a Neo-Renaissance wing of 1657. The Elizabethan wing was the addition made by Roland Vaux. Over the entrance are the arms of the Vaux family quartering those of the Delamores within a circular band which bears the words 'Let Mercy and Faithfulness never go from thee.' In the angles of the panel are the initials of Roland and Anne Vaux, and a short inscription with the date 1577.

The last of the Vaux family to hold Catterlen was John Vaux, who died with no male heir in 1642, so that the manor and Hall descended to his two daughters, Mabel and Mary; the former married Christopher Richmond of Highhead Castle some five years later. He was responsible for adding the Renaissance wing to the Hall. This was approached by sixteen steps from the courtyard.

Catterlen remained in the Richmond family or their descendants until it was sold to the Duke of Norfolk in 1794. The Howards in turn sold it at the beginning of this century.

Newton Reigny

As the Hall is situated about a mile south of the village, and apart from its being on the Catterlen side of the Petteril, it is very much closer to the neighbouring village of Newton Reigny, it is not surprising that in 1934 the two places were united.

The 'New Village' was held in 1185 by William de Reigni, and in 1212 the holder was John de Reingy, who was described at the time as a descendant of Turstan de Reingny, who had been granted the manor by Henry I. The fate of the de Reignys remains unknown, but in the early years of Edward I's reign the manor was held by Robert Burnell, the Bishop of Bath and Wells, 'by service of finding an esquire to serve in the king's army against Scotland, with a haubergeon and an iron helmet, 'at his own cost, for a period of forty days'. In 1290 Bishop Burnell conveyed the manor to Hugh de Lowther.

The first thing anyone visiting Newton Reigny notices is the very wide street, with attractive houses standing right back on either side. There are the Sun and the George III inns and St John's Church with no stained-glass windows, so that again one gets the impression of space. The interior of St John's is late twelfth century, though extensive work was carried out in 1876 by the architect Ewan Christian. An interesting feature may be seen on one of the old beams in the nave where two of the sixteenth-century carpenters, John Atkenson and Henry Bymert, have carved their names and the date, 1585.

Near to Newton Reigny, about a mile south-east of the village, is the Newton Rigg College of Agriculture and Forestry. A mile or so due south of this what is called the Greystoke Pillar stands in a field beside the Greystoke Road, the B5288, and bearing the Arms of the Greystoke family marks the boundary of the barony of Greystoke and the Honour of Penrith.

It is now time to move northwards, to take the direction of the River Petteril, which runs parallel with the M6 motorway and the A6 and the main London to Carlisle Railway. All is moving towards Carlisle, but there are many things to see on the way, particularly the fine house at Hutton-in-the-Forest.

Hutton-in-the-Forest

Hutton is 'the village on the spur of land' from the Old English '*hoh*' meaning a heel or ridge end, and it is, of course, within the confines of Inglewood Forest. 'Hoton in foresta' appears in records as early as 1235, and Thomas de Hoton in Foresta held the manor from 1272 until 1307. It seems the de Hotons had the responsibility for maintaining the forest, for in 1343 Thomas de Hoton 'was restored to the bailiwick and office of keeping the King's lands at Plumpton', and in 1393 William de Hoton held the office of maintaining the palings or fences of the King's forest at Plumpton. The mention of 'palings' may remind us that Hutton-in-the-Forest Hall began as a 'palinged tower' or 'pele tower', the name deriving from the enclosure fence that surrounded the tower, rather than the tower itself.

In 1544 William Hutton (note the change in spelling) held the manor *in capite* by knight's service, and in the latter years of the sixteenth century 'the low two-storeyed building against the southern face of the tower was added'.

It was in 1605 that Lancelot Hutton sold the hall to Sir Richard Fletcher of Cockermouth, who greatly altered the building and filled in the moat. Later additions were made by the Fletchers, and a 'spacious gallery' was built by Sir George Fletcher in 1640; he is said to have asked Inigo Jones to make plans and design the pigeon house, so that in 1675 Hutton was described as a 'princelike palace'.

In 1790 a great storm caused much damage to the house, but by 1806 its buildings and plantations were 'now one of the pleasantest seats in the country'. 'The estate is within the Hay of Plumpton, and held of the King by service of holding the King's stirrup when he mounts his horse in his castle of Carlisle.'

Hutton was to pass out of the direct line of the Fletcher family when Sir Henry Fletcher became a Catholic and entered the Benedictine monastery at Douai in Flanders, where he died – the male line of the elder branch died with him. Before he departed for Douai, Sir Henry settled all his property on a distant relative, Thomas Fletcher of Moresby, 'reserving only for himself a small competency for life'. After his death, his sisters, as heirs at law, commenced a suit in Chancery for the whole estate. A compromise was reached whereby Thomas Fletcher should enjoy Hutton during his lifetime but, should he die without children, the estate should go to Henry Fletcher Vane, nephew of the late Sir Henry. Today Hutton is the home of Lord Inglewood, and it is open to the public each Thursday from the end of May until September.

The little church of St James is situated on the north side of the Wigton road and stands rather on its own. It was built in 1714.

In 1934 Hutton-in-the-Forest was added to Skelton parish, a village about two miles to the west of it, but before I go on to speak of Skelton, there is a small hamlet between the two with the strange name of Unthank. Many will have wondered, as I have, what the name means. It is the Old English word '*unþanc*' meaning ill-will or displeasure and denoted a place which was held against the will of the rightful owner. It seems that squatters were not unusual even in 1254, when the name first appears. There is another Unthank in Addingham Parish.

Skelton takes its name from the small hill on which it is situated, from the Old English '*scylf*', meaning a shelf or ledge of land. There are six places with the same name in Yorkshire. Skelton parish originally consisted of three townships, Skelton itself, Lamonby and Unthank. The manor was held by the Boyvill family from the time of Henry II, but Skelton was eventually divided into six when the six sisters of Randolph Boyvill inherited portions of the manor. The eldest sister, Euphemia, was the wife of Richard Kirkbride, whose descendants continued to hold their share for six generations. The details of the various to-ings and fro-ings of many families in relationship to the divisions of the manor make very dull reading; suffice it to say that the Duke of Devonshire eventually came to hold part of Skelton.

St Michael's Church, with its attractive medieval west tower, was restored in 1879. In 1347 a charter was granted for a chantry dedicated to the Blessed Virgin Mary to be established in the church, but it 'did not then take effect'; however, such a foundation was subsequently endowed with land in Skelton and elsewhere. The existence of the chantry may account for Bishop Nicholson's recording that Skelton church was dedicated to St Mary.

It would have been a happy conclusion to this chapter had the seventeenth-century Oxford antiquary Anthony à Wood been able to give more than a hint that the Tudor poet John Skelton was born in Cumberland. Samuel Jefferson in his *The History and Antiquities of the Leath Ward in the County of Cumberland* includes Skelton among his biographies of eminent 'worthies'. There is no way of telling the truth in the matter, but it has been assumed that Skelton was born in Norfolk and that, when he became rector of Diss in 1498, he was returning to his own county. However, there is the name to consider, and that would imply Cumberland in Yorkshire, as we have seen. Perhaps in honour of the place, if not in one of her famous sons, I might be excused the indulgence of finishing with one of the many 'Skeltonic' maidens, not his more famous Margery but:

Merry Margaret,
    As midsummer flower,
  Gentle as falcon
  Or hawk of the tower:
With solace and gladness,
Much mirth and no madness,
All good and no badness ...

9

The East Fellside

'I have one of the greatest stags of the forest.'
Earl of Huntingdon, 1593

It is the great escarpment of the eastern fells of Westmorland and Cumberland that will dominate the landscape from now on, for the bastion of the Pennines forming a background to the Eden Valley has many villages and hamlets situated beside the small streams that race down towards the greater river. Many people who do not know the villages may well know their names, because the names are also given to the fells high above them: Murton, Dufton, Knock, Milburn, Kirkland and Skirwith Fells are names familiar to those who walk the Pennine Way.

The escarpment stretches in a more or less north-easterly direction from Stainmore to Brampton, in Cumberland, and beyond. What one sees from the valley is a series of fells of differing heights and degrees of shape and smoothness. The celebrated Pennine Fault is, in fact, a whole series of fractures which has resulted in Knock and Dufton Pikes, like Murton Pike on their southern side, being separated from the main block of the Pennines, forming what is known as the Cross Fell Inlier. ('Inlier' is the name given to any place where an old type of rock is surrounded by younger.) Dufton and Knock Pikes are conical-shaped fells, as might be expected from their names, since '*pic*' in Old English meant a point, or pointed hill. These pikes stand as small pawns to the royal figures of the fells rising very much higher behind them. Here the names are repeated, so that we find Dufton and Knock Fells, and beyond them Milburn Forest and Skirwith Fell, beside which is the highest point in all this range, Cross Fell, rising to 2,930 feet. Although Cross Fell is the highest point, it is not the most interesting for the geologist. The pride of place must be granted to the stratum of exposed Whinstone at High Cup Gill. High Cup Nick, as it is called, is not sedimentary rock, like the Pennines generally, but an example of igneous or volcanic rock, which a glacier has unearthed. No doubt there is much more of it hidden beneath the surface of the Eden Valley. The hard black stone, known as Whin Sill, is starkly contrasted with the lighter colour of the limestone that surrounds it.

Now this has not been a guide for walkers, neither is it about to become one; other writers have covered the ground on the fell-tops well enough. It is the small villages at the feet of the fells that interest me, although I have been conscious of those great heights as I have walked around the small river valleys. By the banks of the Leith and the Lyvennet, and particularly the Eamont, I kept having glimpses of Cross Fell as I ascended each small hill, only to lose it as I dropped down again. The fells were not, however, a constant part of my journey, and often they were veiled in cloud or mist, but those masses of rising rock are always in the mind: local flocks graze upon them, great winds gust down from them, and water accumulated on their slopes and racing down their gills gullies by. Sadly, I shall not be able to speak of them all with the same degree of detail – that would require another full-length book – but each has some points of interest. On the map these fellside villages appear to be in two lines, particularly the villages that are situates in old Westmorland. Those nearer to the fells are Dufton, Knock and Milburn, which link naturally with Blencarn and Skirwith across the old Cumberland border, and those closer to the Eden and the A66 are Crackenthorpe, Long Marton, Kirkby Thore and Temple Sowerby, where a minor road, the B6412, leads off northwards towards Culgaith. Between these two lines of villages the Settle to Carlisle railway line runs on its penultimate stretch from Appleby to Langwathby, by way of Long Marton, Newbiggin and Culgaith. Of course, the talk of 'lines' is a little misleading, and it is probably the railway and the very red-looking main road that put the idea into one's head. In fact, the villages are so situated because of water and, to a lesser extent, shelter. Knock, Dufton, Brampton, Long Marton and Kirkby Thore are all dependent on Trout Beck and its tributaries, Swindale Beck and Great Rundale Beck; Milburn and Newbiggin are situated by Milburn Beck and Crowdundle Beck, while Temple Sowerby has its own small stream, which passes the large house, Acorn Bank, before it meets Milburn Beck. Only Culgaith lacks its own stream, but its growth in importance was largely owing to the railway and its famous tunnel.

The most southerly in all this group is Crackenthorpe, where we should watch our steps, because the name seems to mean 'the settlement or hamlet of one who walks with difficulty'. There are other Crackenthorpes in the north, one fairly close at Beetham, near Kendal, and another, spelt slightly differently, at Caton, in Lancashire. It is likely that the Old Norse 'Krakandi' was some kind of byname and referred to a particular person early associated with the place. The name first appears in a twelfth-century document and is spelt 'Crakantorp'.

Situated two miles north-west of Appleby, Crackenthorpe saw a great change when the A66 was widened; originally the main Appleby to Penrith road ran through the village street, but now the busy run of traffic cuts the village in two so that the Hall stands on its own. Although the building has an impressive front, the main windows look out from the village towards the Eden and the point where Hoff Beck joins it by Colby.

The manor of Crackenthorpe was held by the Machell family from Norman times, though the circumstances of their coming to the place are unknown. The name of the family in early documents was often written 'Malus Catulus', and several members appear before Roger Malus Catulus is mentioned as Vice-Chancellor of England at the time of Richard I; accompanying his sovereign on the Third Crusade, he was drowned off the coast of Cyprus. As William Whellan says in his

The History and Topography of the Counties of Cumberland and Westmorland, published in 1840, 'The antiquity of this family is beyond dispute, and can be established by family papers, 'but the exploits of the different members are hard to discover. Guy and Hugh Machell accompanied Henry VIII to France and took part in the siege of Tournai. At the time of the Restoration of Charles II, Lancelot Machell, first mayor of Appleby since the Commonwealth, 'destroyed in open court, Cromwell's charter, before he took office'. Such behaviour would suggest a healthy mind. As far as Westmorland is concerned, the most illustrious member of the Machell family was Thomas Machell, the antiquary, of whom I shall speak in connection with Kirkby Thore, where he was rector. Thomas Machell was born at Crackenthorpe Hall in 1647, the second son of the charter-destroying Lancelot.

Crackenthorpe Hall was built, probably on the site of an earlier building, during the lifetime of Thomas Machell, and it seems he had a hand in helping his brother refront and recondition the house in 1685. However, the Hall was said to have been rebuilt first in 1629 and again altered in 1663.

It is Lingard, in his *History of England*, published in 1819, who mentions that Henry VI took refuge at Crackenthorpe after the battle of Hexham, in 1464. It seems this was not a hiding-place on one visit only, for Lingard says, 'He was during this time frequently concealed in the house of John Machell, at Crackenthorpe, in Westmorland.' The people of that county and Lancashire, Lingard goes on to note, were 'sincerely devoted to his interests. Their fidelity enabled him for more than a year to elude the vigilance and researches of the government.' Of course, Lingard means the Yorkist government.

What is often referred to as the Roman camp at Crackenthorpe is situated well over a mile away, north-west of the village, and, in fact, is very much nearer to Bolton. The site is cut across by the main road and the road to Long Marton, and is only some fifty yards from the old Roman road which is marked clearly on the Ordnance Survey map of the Appleby area. The camp, of which almost nothing worth seeing remains, covered an area of about twenty-two acres and is similar to that at Rey Cross, near Brough.

The road to Long Marton leads from the site of the camp to the small hamlet of Brampton and to Dufton, besides Long Marton itself. Brampton is one of the townships of Long Marton, though it was a manor in its own right and was held by the Greystoke family as early as the reign of Edward II, and they continued to possess it until 1422. After that date Brampton passed to the Lancasters of Sockbridge, 'by whom the manor was held of the Greystokes, as the latter held it of the Cliffords, by homage, fealty, and scutage'. When the Lancaster family ended in three daughters during the reign of Elizabeth I, Brampton was divided between their respective husbands, a Birbeck of Hornby, a Backhouse of Morland and a Wharton of Kirkby Thore. Subsequently the Birbeck part of the manor was exchanged with the Earl of Thanet, the heir to the Clifford estates, for land at Hornby.

Brampton is 'the farmstead amongst the broom', and the next village, Dufton is 'the farmstead where doves were kept'; the spelling has remained constant since the twelfth century, and there is no doubt whatsoever as to the meaning, but how Dufton came by the name there is no way of telling. If it is remembered that every large estate would have had a dovecote in medieval times, it is not difficult to imagine that Dufton was particularly well known for its pigeons, and perhaps the birds for the tables of Appleby Castle or Crackenthorpe Hall were brought down the road through Brampton.

The Greystoke family are the first recorded possessors of Dufton after the Norman Conquest, but nothing is known prior to that time. In 1335, during Edward III's regin, Ralph de Greystoke held the manors of Dufton, Brampton, Bolton and Yanwath, but these had been granted to him by the Cliffords. The Greystokes continued to hold Dufton until the reign of Henry VIII, when Elizabeth Greystoke married Thomas, Lord Dacre of Gilsland, and brought Dufton into that family. From the Dacres it passed to the Howards.

It may be remembered that Anne Dacre had married Philip Howard, the eldest son of the Duke of Norfolk. In the partition of the estates Dufton became her property. But what she could not have foreseen was that her husband's name would be closely linked with a young man who was born in Dufton in 1543, John Boste: Philip Howard and John Boste were among the Forty Martyrs of England and Wales canonized by Pope Paul VI in 1970.

John Boste, pronounced 'Boast', came from a family that practised the 'Old Religion'. There is no definite evidence that he attended Appleby Grammar School but, it being the nearest and a grammar school education being mentioned in one account of his life, it may be fairly assumed that he went there. He went on to become a Fellow of Queen's College, Oxford, in 1572, where he was ordained into the recently established Church of England.

Exactly when Boste decided to revert to the faith of his family is not known, but he crossed the seas to be admitted into the seminary founded by Cardinal Allen, which had moved from Douai to Rheims. He was ordained a priest in the Catholic Church in 1581, and on 11 April that year he set out for the English Mission, landing at Hartlepool. For the next twelve years he worked hard as a missionary priest, risking his life on many occasions, and so successful was he that he became a marked man. For many years the priest-hunters under the command of the Earl of Huntingdon were on his track. Boste was eventually betrayed by the treachery of an informer who had pretended to be a zealous Catholic, and after offering Mass at a place called Waterhouse, about four miles west of Durham, he was captured on 10 September 1593. The news of his capture so delighted Huntingdon that he made the well-known statement: 'I have one of the greatest stags of the forest.'

Boste was examined at Durham, taken to York and, later, so important was he considered, escorted to London, where he was severely tortured and racked, with the result that he was never again able to walk properly. He was nine months in the Tower and on one occasion was taken as a curiosity to be inspected by the Queen. Eventually he was returned to the north, where he was tried and sentenced to death. Boste was hanged, drawn and quartered at Durham on 24 July 1594. According to one eye-witness account of the martyrdom, after disembowelling the victim the hangman tore out the heart and held it up with the words: 'Behold the heart of a traitor.' At which a voice from the crowd was heard to reply: 'No, the heart of a servant of God.'

Long Marton

Long Marton is really 'Meretun', 'the farmstead with a pool or mere'. It appears frequently in early records as 'Merton' and is not described as 'Long' until the sixteenth century, probably because it is a long-shaped parish extending from Knock northwards and southwards to Brampton. In 1272 there was mention of '*parvum vivarium de Merton*', 'the small fishpool of Merton', so it seems that Merton was the place where fish were fed for the table, just as Dufton was the place for pigeons.

Marton belonged first to the Veteripont family during the reign of Henry III, afterwards to the Cliffords, by whom it was held during the reigns of Edward III and Richard II. Then it passed to the Hollands, and Sir John de Holland is recorded as holding the manor in the fifteenth year of Richard II's reign, 1392. During the reigns of Henry V and Henry VI it was held by the Gray family, but by some means or other it fell into the hands of Henry VIII. Presumably the Gray estates became forfeit to the Crown; whether this was because of their part in the Pilgrimage of Grace, I have not been able to find out, but I suspect this to have been the case.

The delightful little church of St Margaret and St James at Long Marton is one of the best-preserved parish churches in the district, since it was not 'messed about' by the Victorians and so much of the original Norman work remains. The west tower is twelfth century, for instance. However, I do not mean to say that no work was carried out in the last century, but that it was done with a great sense of the past. When in 1874 the Reverend Hay Macdonald Erskine became rector, it was a boon for the parish, because being a man of means he was able to employ the best in design and building skill. The architect engaged was John Cory, and the partnership of Cory and Ferguson was as celebrated as the more ubiquitous Paley and Austin. Their best work is seen at St Cuthbert's, Plumbland, but there they were starting from scratch. At Long Marton they had a substantial church to restore, and even the modern chancel arch merges in successfully with the older nave. Inside the church there is a fine thirteenth-century chest, but many interesting items also, including a window to the good Mr Erskine, who remained rector of Long Marton until 1896. The church is situated a little distance south of the village, where there is one of the few thatched cottages in the area.

Knock

Like Brampton, Knock is one of the townships of Long Marton, situated some two miles north-west of Dufton and separated from Long Marton by Marton Moor. The name comes from the Celtic word '*chocc*', meaning a hillock; there is a well-known place of the same name in the west of Ireland, where there is a shrine to the Blessed Virgin Mary. Indeed, when Pope John Paul II, visited England, Father Walsh, now the parish priest of St Catherine's, Penrith, expressed the happy hope that the helicopter pilot might land at the wrong Knock. Presumably the name refers to the prominent hill, Knock Pike, north of the village, though here as in many Westmorland place-names there is an unnecessary repetition.

Knock has grown up between two becks, of which Swindale Beck, 'the beck of the valley of the wild swine', is the larger. It is a much smaller village than Dufton, really little more than a hamlet.

In several records of the fourteenth century the manor appears as 'Knock Shalcock', which implies some early ownership, but nothing is known of the Shalcock family in this connection beyond various speculations. What is known is that the Cliffords granted Knock to the Boyvilles, Rookbys, Soulbys and Lancasters in turn, until it was maintained by the Cliffords, whose descendants are still Lords of the Manor.

St Cuthbert's Church stands on the east side of the road from Dufton to Knock and is officially Dufton parish church, since Knock was always part of Long Marton. There has been a church on this site since before the Norman Conquest, for it is known that Dufton, like Cliburn and Clifton, was mentioned by Prior Wessington in 1416 as being one of the places where the monks of Lindisfarne, fleeing from the Danes in the year 875, had rested. The Prior was recording 'strong tradition'; what is certain is that the monks were carrying with them two important holy relics: the incorrupt body of St Cuthbert and the head of St Oswald. Those places where the body of St Cuthbert rested had churches built and dedicated to him. The first record in existence concerning the church is of 1293, when one of its rectors is mentioned.

What may be seen today is the west tower built in 1784 and the thorough restoration of 1853, but much, if not most, of the masonry is very old.

Kirkby Thore

For those who do not live in the area, Kirkby Thore may be best known through British Gypsum, the large firm that mines the light grey deposit of gypsum-anhydrite at various places along the Eden Valley. At Kirkby Thore their factory makes plaster and plaster-board in what is described as 'one of the most advanced factories in the world'. For those particularly interested in the geology of the Penrith area, I would recommend *Geology of the Country around Penrith*, published by Her Majesty's Stationery Office in 1981.

However, it is history that concerns me, and Kirkby Thore is exceptionally important in that regard. It was very well known to the Romans, whose station there was called Bravoniacum. The name means either 'the place of querns' or 'the estate of Bravonius'. The station was situated a little north of the intersection between two Roman roads: the main route from Stainmore to Brougham, and the road from Casterton which ran up the Lune valley passing Low Borrow Bridge and followed a course through the ancient settlement of Ewe Close near Crosby Ravensworth and thence to Kirkby Thore. Once the road left Kirkby Thore, it continued over Melmerby Fell to Alston, crossing Crowdundle Beck on the way. This later part of the road was known as Maiden Way in medieval times. It is mentioned in 1179 in the records of Holm Cultram Abbey, where it is written as 'Maydengathe', the maiden's road. It is in the same record of the date 1179 that the first spelling of Kirkby Thore is found: 'the village with a church' belonging to Thorir, the name of an early owner about whom nothing is known. Any suggestion that the

Norse god of Thunder was worshipped in the place, or that he was particularly venerated there, seems far fetched, but it is mentioned in Bulmer's *Directory of Westmorland* as a possibility, and it is indeed possible that there was a temple to Thor in the village.

During the reign of King Stephen, Kirkby Thore is mentioned as a manor held by a certain Whelph, who is reputed to have been the father of the Gamel whose son Waldeve donated certain lands in the area of the abbey at Holm Cultram. In the early twelfth century Whelp is thought to have built a castle on the site of the old Roman fort, whose site may still be seen. Here in 1687 the rector of the parish, Thomas Machell, carried out certain excavations and unearthed 'a four-fold wall made of hewn stone, each wall being two feet four inches thick'. Machell also found several vaulted arches and yards of lead piping together with a Roman altar bearing the inscription '*Fortune Servatrici*' on the site; near the bridge and the Roman road he discovered a well containing several urns, earthen vessels, the clasp of a spear and sandals. (In damp conditions leather deteriorates little, and our museums contain many exhibits of armour leather, shoes and tents. There are several pieces of Roman tent on show at Carlisle.)

This would seem the right place to say a little more about the remarkable antiquary Thomas Machell, whose observations so carefully recorded with simple sketches and diagrams have provided the basis of much of our knowledge of the county of Westmorland. It was largely on Machell's notes that Richard Burn and Joseph Nicolson drew for their knowledge of the county in their *The History and Antiquities of Westmorland and Cumberland*, published in 1777. Machell was seeing things some century earlier.

Thomas Machell was the second son of Lancelot Machell, the owner of Crackenthorpe Hall, for long the family home. He was born there in 1647. Little is known of his early years, but it seems fairly certain that he was a pupil at Appleby Grammar School and that he went up to Queen's College, Oxford, at the age of sixteen. In 1668 he became Bachelor of Arts, and in March 1671 Master of Arts, becoming a year later a Fellow of the college. It was while he was up at Oxford that the idea of making a detailed study of his own county was formed. This was largely owing to his meeting there two famous antiquaries, Sir William Dugdale, who had made a study of Warwickshire, and Anthony à Wood. 'I am conscious of mine own inabilities to perform such a work as Mr Dugdale's having neither the leisure nor ingenuity,' he informed Sir Daniel Fleming at Rydal.

On 15 August 1677 Machell was inducted as rector of Kirkby Thore, and it was from there that he set out on his many excursions round the county on horseback, notebook at the ready. Machell's time as rector was not without difficulties. The previous incumbent had been slack, and the parish had been allowed to run down. The meticulous mind of Machell set all in order. The rectory was repaired, besides the church, and Machell presented new furnishings for the latter: a Communion table and rail and a new pulpit and font.

At first Machell had thought to write his historical notes from information that others might give him, writing off to distinguished men living in the different parishes, 'Gentlemen and Ministers of the Countrey' from whom he hoped to receive the 'greatest assistance'. This method proved disappointing, and thank goodness for it, because Machell's decision to go to see for himself and make sketches on the spot means far more to us than any amount of description. His fact-finding journeys began in 1678 and continued during the years until his death in 1693.

Machell was honoured by his contemporaries, becoming a Doctor of Divinity and Fellow of the Royal Society, besides being Fellow of the Oxford Philosophical Society, and when King Charles II appointed him one of his chaplains in ordinary, it was a fitting reward for this conscientious and, one senses, holy man.

The reputation of Machell seems destined to increase. The six volumes of notes in manuscript are lodged in the Dean and Chapter Library at Carlisle. His handwriting is exceedingly difficult to decipher in many instances but his sketches provide invaluable evidence. There remains much work to be done, although Jane M. Ewbank undertook invaluable work on the second volume of the notes dealing with the Barony of Kendal. This was published in 1963 as *Antiquary on Horseback*.

Machell's church at Kirkby Thore dedicated to St Michael the Archangel is well worth a visit. It was designed in the early English style with a nave, chancel and side aisles, but there is evidence of Norman work in the chancel arch and in that of the north window. The west tower, which has decorated bell-openings, was built in the twelfth century but has had a seventeenth-century gabled bell-cote added. The single bell, thought to have been cast in York in about 1450, is said to have been brought from Shap Abbey after the Dissolution. There is no evidence for this supposition beyond the fact that the last abbot of Shap, Richard Evenwode, became rector of Kirkby Thore. However, in the event it seems quite likely that the good abbot retrieved his bell at least.

Temple Sowerby

The old name of this manor lacked the prefix 'Temple', and several persons are on record who derived their name from the place. There is mention of Adam de Soureby and William de Soureby, but no indication of whether they held property there. Neither is it certain at what date the Knights Templar came to hold the manor, but 'Temple' was prefixed to the name in a document in 1279, well over a hundred years after the Knights had come to England.

The Templars, whose full title was the Poor Knights of Christ and the Temple of Solomon, were a religious military order established at the time of the Crusades. The Crusaders who founded the kingdom of Jerusalem had only slight control of the main pilgrim route, with the result that there was continual harassment from marauding bands of Muslims. Seeing the need for maintaining safety along the route, a group of French knights, only some nine or ten in number, under the leadership of Hugues de Payens, vowed in 1120 to devote their lives to the task and to live in community for that purpose. The quarters granted to them by Baldwin II, King of Jerusalem, were in part of the palace which occupied a portion of the area of the former Jewish Temple – hence the name they adopted.

The rule of life adopted by the knights was drawn up for them by St Bernard of Clairvaux and sanctioned by the Council of

Troyes in 1128. Over the following years the number of knights increased, but so did their duties, which extended beyond protecting pilgrims to providing a ready army able to fight for the cause of Christianity in any part of the world where the infidel was threatening. The order became exceedingly rich through many endowments from all over Europe. Its emphasis on absolute secrecy to cover all their internal activities has meant that it is often seen, quite wrongly, as the forerunner of other groups, particularly of the Freemasons, whose rites of initiation are also a closely guarded secret.

The other religio-military order, and the elder of the two, was the Order of the Knights of St John of Jerusalem, known more generally as Hospitallers, which had been founded during the eleventh century by the merchants of Amalfi to provide shelter and protection for the pilgrims. Although both orders took monastic vows, their main function was soldiering, and once they were established, like any other religious order, they began to grow. Soon they were established all over Europe. They were 'virtually independent, sanctioned and continually supported by the Papacy'. Perhaps the greatest resentment the Knights aroused in the popular mind at the time was their exemption from local ecclesiastical jurisdiction. The clergy were thus jealous of them, and they constituted a serious challenge to royal authority. The power of the Templars was seen as a threat by Philip IV, known as 'Philip the Fair', of France, who in the early years of the fourteenth century decided to bring about the order's downfall.

When the Gascon Pope Clement V moved the Holy See to Avignon and the College of Cardinals became dominated by Frenchmen, it was not too difficult for the French King to get his own way. Accusing the Knights of heresy and immorality, Philip persuaded Pope Clement V to suppress the order, which he did on 22 March 1312. Two years later the Grand Master, Jacques de Molay, was burned at the stake, and in this ignominious way the order ceased. The end of the Knights Templar is described in the *Catholic Encyclopaedia* as follows:

With this pliant pope the way was clear for the strangest act of

> violence and destruction. The Templars were aged men whose privileges seemed poorly justified after the fall of the Holy Land. But Philip's case was pressed relentlessly beyond the evidence brought forth; the king had to resort to propaganda in a vast assembly held at Tour in 1308, and it was only in 1312 that the pope, his scruples overcome by expediency, dissolved the order. The Templars' possessions were given to the Hospitallers, and their last dignitaries were imprisoned or executed.

This meant that Temple Sowerby, one of the townships of Kirkby Thore parish, was held by the Hospitallers until that order was in turn suppressed in England by Henry VIII in 1540.

Certainly the prefix 'Temple' gives this Sowerby a distinguished name. There are other Sowerbys: Castle Sowerby and Brough Sowerby, not so far away. 'Sowerby' means 'the farmstead on muddy or sour ground'; the name is derived from the Old Norse word '*saur*', meaning mud.

Temple Sowerby is familiar to all those who travel along the A66 towards Penrith: the well-appointed inn, the King's Arms, standing back from the road, and the small church, St James's, built in 1754, enlarged in 1770 and again restored in 1873. The road leading off the main road past the church and the attractive village green leads to the large house of the village, Acorn Bank, which is today a Sue Ryder Home. The house was built between 1730 and 1750, incorporating much of an earlier Jacobean building.

Newbiggin

Newbiggin is 'the new settlement', and there are several places with the name in Cumberland and Westmorland, one of which we have seen near Greystoke. I have a particular interest as I am writing this book at Newbiggin-on-Lune. Several of my acquaintances from the south have found themselves at the wrong Newbiggin and telephoned me from Kirkby Thore, having successfully found *a* Newbiggin on the map after travelling up the A1. Of all the Newbiggins, however, the one near Kirkby Thore is the grandest.

Although the manor of Newbiggin is on record as having been held by Gamel, the son of a wild-sounding man called Whelp, who granted it to Robert, steward of Appleby, who in consequence assumed the name of Robert de Newbiggin, it is with the Crackenthorpe family that the place is associated. But they would never have appeared on the scene had not a descendant of Robert de Newbiggin, a girl named Emma, married into the Crackenthorpe family. This was in about 1331, when already there was probably some kind of defensive tower in existence at what would later become Newbiggin Hall.

The tower at Newbiggin Hall, known as 'the Jerusalem', was built shortly after the battle of Towton in 1461 'as a refuge for the Crackenthorpe family while the East or pele tower was in ruins'. However, most of what one may see today is a nineteenth-century rebuilding of the house Christopher Crackenthorpe had built in 1533.

Christopher Crackenthorpe men did me call
Who in my time did build this hall,
And framed it as you may see,
One thousand five hundred thirty and three.

It was as 'Christopher Crackenthorpe' that Christopher Cookson, Wordsworth's 'Uncle Kit', took up his residence at the Hall when he inherited in 1792, dropping the Cookson name. His stay at Newbiggin was to be short-lived, for he died suddenly in 1799, unmourned by his nephew, who had found it impossible to forgive him over a sum of £500 presented by Dorothy (Granny) Cookson to Uncle Kit's bride Charlotte Cust in 1788. Wordsworth felt that the money should have been given to the orphaned Wordsworth children. To give Uncle Kit his due, he did leave Dorothy Wordsworth £100 in his will, with which she and her brother were able to furnish their cottage at Grasmere, but brother William could never bring himself to visit Newbiggin.

Christopher Crackenthorpe's son, William, who had been born in 1790, came into the property; he was High Sheriff of Cumberland in 1826. At his death the Hall passed to Montague Cookson Crackenthorpe. Of all the Crackenthorpes perhaps the most interesting was Hubert, born in 1865. He was one of the contributors to the first number of *The Yellow Book* in 1894, the magazine famous for Beardsley's drawings, intended to bring about a renaissance in art and ideas. Crackenthorpe's life was to be very short, dying in 1896 at the early age of thirty-one, but he had made his mark on the literary world of the time as the author of *Vignettes*, a book of travel sketches, and *Wreckage*, one of the first Impressionistic novels, and as editor of the magazine *The Albemarle*, which predated *The Yellow Book* by some two years. He spent most of life in London, but I have seen a photograph of him taken at Newbiggin.

The Crackenthorpe family was responsible for restoring the fine little church next to the Hall, dedicated to St Edmund. The early Norman building was repaired in 1804 and more or less completely rebuilt in 1853-4. One of the best features is the east window, which has fragments of fourteenth-century stained glass. Whether or not these fragments are indigenous to the building is open to doubt, since the Crackenthorpes had done particularly well at the time of the Reformation and bought the house and lands 'which formerly belonged to the Carmelite Friars at Appleby'. Indeed, Newbiggin itself was bought from the Crown by Christopher Crackenthorpe, whose ancestor, Lawrence de Newbiggin, 'for the salvation of his soul and the soul of his wife, had given it to the Abbey of Holme Cultram'.

Christopher Crackenthorpe had also purchased Hale Grange, situated about a mile and a half south-east of the village, and on the opposite side of the railway line there is a small farm called Low Abbey – both signs of the abbey's holding of the land, for the monasteries had 'grange farms' in many places, often a long way from the mother-house, where a few monks would organize the farm and protect the abbot's interests in the area.

It is time to speak of the dreaded Helm Wind, as the next village, Milburn, is one of the line of places most subject to it. 'Helm' means hilltop, so the wind that blows along the Pennines from Brough to Brampton is a hilltop wind such as is known in no other part of the country – a cold, mercilessly violent, easterly wind which howls down from the western slopes of the fells. When the 'Helm' is blowing, a very heavy bank of cloud, known as 'the Helm Cloud', lies along the range, while some three or four miles from the foot of the Fell there is usually, though not always, a slender rolling or whirling cloud. This is 'the Helm Bar' which appears in mid-air and lies parallel with the Helm Cloud. The force of the wind is sometimes so fierce that animals are in danger, and it was known in the old days of horse-drawn vehicles for horses and carts to be blown off the roads. This fierceness can last for three or four days in the spring, but there have been occasions when the wind has lasted, on and off, for as long as three weeks. There is a similar kind of wind that blows at Cape Town in South Africa.

> When t'Helm low, and foxes bark,
> Bar up your door afore it's dark.

The villages of Milburn, Kirkland, Ousby, Melmerby and Gamblesby are most subject of the Helm Wind, but the more distant from the highest point, the less it is felt. The cause of wind is the difference in temperature between the height of the Pennines and the Eden Valley. It was well described by Dr Barnes of Carlisle in the 1840s:

> The air or wind from the east ascends the gradual slope of the eastern side of the Pennine Chain or Cross Fell range of mountains, to the summit of Cross Fell, where it enters the Helm or Cap, and is cooled to a low temperature; it then rushes forcibly down the abrupt declivity of the western side of the mountain into the valley beneath, in consequence of the valley being of a warmer temperature, and this constitutes the Helm Wind. The sudden and violent rushing of the wind down the ravines and crevices of the mountains occasions the loud noise that is heard. At a varying distance from the base of the mountain the Helm wind is rarified by the warmth of the low ground, and meets with the wind from the west, which resists its further course. The higher temperature it has acquired in the valley, and the meeting of the contrary current, occasion it to rebound and ascend into the upper region of the atmosphere.

Milburn

'Milburn' is simply 'the mill stream', but there must have been a very early mill situated on the beck there since the first record of the name occurs in 1178 and appears in the Wetheral Priory Register in the 1220s.

Haytiming near Cliburn

Thomas Bland's Image Garden

High Cup Nick

St Michael's – Addingham

Kirkoswald

St Cuthbert's – Great Salkeld

The village green – Melmerby

Alston

Cross Fell and a bridge on the Settle to Carlisle railway near Langwathby

MAUGHANBY
GAMBLESBY 2
ALSTON 12
Little Salkeld 1½
Langwathby 3
Penrith 8
GLASSONBY
LAZONBY
ROBBERBY 1
HUNSONBY

In the reign of King John, the Forest of Milburn was granted to William de Stuteville, and it was held by that family until Nicholas de Stuteville transferred it to Robert de Veteripont, who gave his grange at Milburn to the canons of Shap Abbey. All the Veteripont estate passed to the Cliffords, and in 1310 they granted Milburn to Patrick, Earl of Dunbar, 'except the parts previously granted to the Abbey'. Earl Patrick, in the disputes between Edward I and Robert Bruce, 'espoused the cause of his King and countryman, for which loyal act he forfeited his English estates'. Milburn was then granted to a branch of the Lancaster family, 'descended from Roger de Lancaster, illegitimate brother of William de Lancaster, third Baron of Kendal'.

From the Lancaster family the manor passed by marriage of an heiress to Robert de Crackenthorpe, and again through marriage to Sir Thomas Sandford of Askham. Lastly Milburn was given by another marriage to the Honeywoods of Marks Hall, Essex, and Philip Honeywood in 1780 sold the manor to the Earl of Thanet.

Describing the village, Nikolaus Pevsner says it is 'obviously made not grown', referring to the fact that Milburn appears to have been planned. An oblong green is lined on all four sides with rows of cottages and houses, attached to or closely situated by each other. At each of the four corners a road enters; these could easily have been barricaded in the days when the marauding Scots were on the offensive.

The church at Milburn, with its little bellcote dated 1616, the year of Shakespeare's death, is said to have been founded by the monks of Shap Abbey 'for the spiritual benefit of the inmates of their grange at Milburn'. It was endowed with £4 a year, payable by the abbot and the community 'out of the lands given to that house by Robert de Veteripont'. This medieval church was restored in 1788, and again in 1894, when the interior was completely renovated, but much of what may be seen today is original Norman work.

The chief 'monument' of Milburn is situated half a mile away from the village and directly east of it; this is Howgill Castle. The name interests me because at first sight it appears to be the same

The crossroads at Maughanby

as the Howgills, the fells upon which I am looking as I write; but the Milburn 'Howgill' has a different origin, as the earliest records make perfectly clear. It is not the Old Norse '*haugr*', meaning a hill or mound that is the base here, but '*hol*', meaning a hole or hollow. The earliest spelling of the name is 'Hollegill' and the l does not give way to a w until the sixteenth century. The name simply means 'the hollow ravine'.

Originally the castle consisted of twin pele towers built about the years 1375, but there was almost certainly some kind of a building here before that date, in the time of Patrick, Earl of Dunbar, who, as we have seen, sided with Robert Bruce in the wars of Scottish Independence and forfeited Milburn. In 1327 John de Lancaster of Holegill represented Westmorland in Parliament, but his dates are uncertain and the peles were probably built after his time. What is certain is that a hall was built in about 1550, though little of this building remains, and a central block of rooms 'in the Wren tradition' took its place dating from 1733. However, in 1671 Howgill was described as 'a fair stone building, and hath an excellent prospect over a great part of the country. Sir Richard Sandford Bart. is now the owner thereof.' In 1811 it was recorded that, 'The walls were formerly, and some of them are yet ten and a half feet thick. Underneath it were large arched vaultes, for the safe safety of cattle by night against the border moss troopers.'

Kirkland

The ancient parish of Kirkland, 'the church land', originally consisted of two townships, Kirkland with Blencarn, and Skirwith, and the chapelry of Culgaith. Under the terms of the Deanery and Parish Organization of the Diocese of Carlisle which came into effect in 1980, Kirkland was to remain a single parish, while Culgaith was to be united with Edenhall and Langwathby, and Skirwith with Ousby and Melmerby. If one looks at the map, it is easy to see how all this makes sense. In fact, Kirkland itself is fairly insignificant today compared with Culgaith, which developed, as did Langwathby, because of the railway. 'Kirkland' is printed on the map in very small letters, while Culgaith ranks with Greystoke in importance. Kirkland has gained, if anything, remaining a place well worth visiting for its relative remoteness. It is set in beautiful farming countryside backed by the great fells beyond, with a fine old church, St Lawrence's, said to have been in medieval times a much larger building. If one forgoes the gate and climbs up through the stone stile into the churchyard, as most will, there are several good tombs of the Salkeld family to be seen, and an old cross over eight feet high with much of its base intact.

About half a mile from the church, through several gates, one may see the pre-Roman farming terraces, known as 'the Hanging Walls of Mark Antony'. The name seems somewhat incongruous as the terraces are certainly not Roman, and Mark Anthony never visited Britain, but they are situated fairly close to the Roman road, the Maiden Way, and the name was probably a nineteenth-century idea meant to be vaguely Roman and reminiscent of the Hanging Gardens of Babylon.

In 1847 Kirkland was described as a manor 'containing only about fourteen enfranchised tenements holden under Lady le Fleming, of Rydal in Westmorland'. Less is known about Kirkland than about Blencarn, 'the summit crag', with which it has for so long been linked. Blencarn was part of the 'the large barony of Adam fitz Swein, and as such was held by the Neville family'. A portion was subsequently held by the priory of Carlisle, 'in free alms'. During the reign of King John the Whitbys and the Thursbys each held a moiety. In 1226 Evan de Vipont and Sibell Thursby, his wife, gave six bovates of land in Blancarn to Bernard Thursby, and in 1278, he granted a portion of this to the priory of Carlisle. The remainder seems to have been inherited by Edmund Boyville, his second son, who sold it to John Hercla, or Harcla, from whom the portion of the manor was inherited by Sir Andrew de Harcla, a soldier who had served Edward I on his campaigns and been greatly rewarded with the title of Earl of Carlisle and many estates in Cumberland, Westmorland and Yorkshire. Unfortunately, Sir Andrew's new-found wealth was to be short-lived, since he was made the scapegoat when in the next reign he failed to prevent Robert Bruce's invading England in 1323. He was executed at Carlisle, and all his estates were forfeited. Much of his estate was granted by Edward II to Lord Neville of Raby, but Blencarn was granted to William Langley, or English, whose heiress brought it to the Restwolds, from whom it passed to the Lough family. In 1792 the tenants were enfranchised by Lough Carleton, but the memorial rights remained in his family.

Culgaith

The name of the next village, Culgaith, means something like 'the corner wood' and is British in origin. As I have said, the place developed owing to the railway, and the third longest tunnel on the Settle to Carlisle line was dug through the hill on which the village is situated. Although nothing like as long as the tunnels under Blea Moor and Rise Hill, Culgaith is 661 yards long with a single ventilation shaft of seventy-four feet – Blea Moor is some two thousand feet longer.

Culgaith has often been described as a long, straggling village, and it has not the obvious charm of Skirwith, but there is good scenery around it, particularly the road towards Langwathby which takes one past the point where the River Eamont, straight and stately, meets the more meandering Eden.

Culgaith had a good inn, the Black Swan, and a church dedicated to All Saints, built on the site of the earlier chapel-of-ease in 1756 and consecrated two years later. Things did not always go smoothly at Culgaith, however, because in 1456 the Pope issued a commission of inquiry to investigate the fact that weekday Masses were not being offered in the chapel. Perhaps it was too far away for the priest at Kirkland to make the journey more than the obligatory one on a Sunday! The distance was seven miles.

Skirwith

Skirwith is a most attractive village, built along each side of, though high up on, the banks above Skirwith Beck. The beck began at Kirkland Beck and, once past Skirwith, will become Briggle Beck, written 'Brigghill' in 1598, which meets the Eden about a mile and a half north of Langwathby. 'Skirwith' is derived from the same elements as 'Sherwood' and means 'a wood shared in common by a whole district'. It was manorially part of Adam fitz Swein's barony, and after passing through several families it was purchased in 1606 by Agnes, the widow of William Fleming, whose descendant, Sir Michael Fleming, is said to have enfranchised the tenants. The old manor house, known as Skirwith Hall, was demolished in 1795 and a farmhouse erected on the site. However, there is a large house in the village, Skirwith Abbey, said to have been built on land once held by the Knights Templar and described as a 'modern built mansion' in 1802. In 1822 it was bought by William Parker, who did much for the village, building the Sun Inn and 'some neat cottages in the village' and helping to found the school. It is interesting to see that in 1847 Joseph Bewley is listed as 'victualler of the Sun and a schoolmaster'.

The church of St John the Evangelist, designed by Messrs Francis and built in 1856, stands on the south side of the beck. Unfortunately I was unable to go inside because I found it locked. It has a south-west tower with a small spire.

The villages of which I have just written are dominated by the great fells, and particularly by Cross Fell. This was originally Fiend's Fell and is so written in 1340; it may well be some reference to the Helm Wind, Devil's work, if ever there was any. However, early in the seventeenth century Fiend's Fell was appearing as Cross Fell in documents. There would seem from documentary evidence little truth in the tradition that St Paulinus erected a cross and built an altar on the summit, 'where he celebrated Mass, and thus drove away the demons'. I hope sincerely that St Paulinus did just that, but the people were still talking about Fiend's Fell in 1479, and St Paulinus had died in 644.

10

The Road to Alston Moor

> If that cuppe
> Shall break or fall
> Farewell the lucke
> Of Edenhalle.
> Traditional

The Alston road, the A686, begins gently enough from Penrith, soon passing on the left-hand side the house called Carleton Hill, built in 1841 by Frances Trollope, the mother of Anthony Trollope, the author of *Barchester Towers*. Mrs Trollope lived in the house for only two years, but her son visited her there on one or two occasions, travelling up by coach. In one of his novels he describes a coach stopping in Shap just long enough for its occupants to thank Heaven they had not been born 'Shappites'.

Past Carleton Hill and Whinsfield and on towards Langwathby where it crosses the Eden and, a little further on, Buggle Beck which flows parallel with the larger river, meeting it by Little Salkeld some two miles to the north-west, the Alston road bypasses Edenhall, a mile or so before it reaches Langwathby.

It has often been supposed – quite wrongly – that the place takes its name from the mansion, the Hall, for long the home of the Musgrave family. The name is very much older than the Hall and has nothing to do with buildings, 'hall' meaning 'a piece of flat land by the side of a river'. The Old English '*halh*' appears in the northern dialect as 'haugh' is many instances but is more easily seen in Wetheral, Lessonhall and several other names, of which Edenhall is probably the best known.

Edenhall became the home of the Musgraves by marriage as late as 1460, and the Hall itself was designed on the site of an earlier building by Robert Smirke in 1821. It has since been demolished.

The manor of Edenhall was supposedly given to Henry fitz Swein by William Rufus when he came north in 1092. In the reign of Henry III Robert Turp appears in the records as the owner, and it passed by marriage to William Stapleton in 1327. It remained a Stapleton possession for five generations until a Joan Stapleton married Thomas de Musgrave during the reign of Henry VI in 1459.

The Musgraves were indeed a most illustrious family, and it is reasonable to say a little about the family before venturing forth upon their renowned 'Luck'.

Like many families of their kind, the Musgraves are reputed to have come over from Normandy with the Conqueror. According to the editor of *Burke's Peerage*, the family deduced its pedigree from one of the Companions at Arms of William I who received from the Conqueror the grant of Scaleby Castle in Cumberland. However, as I argued in my book on the Howgills, William Camden, in his *Britannia*, published in 1586, describes the family as having taken its name from the two Westmorland villages of Great and Little Musgrave. The name is certainly English and means a mouse-infested wood. Be this as it may, it was common for families to take their names from places, and one thing is certain: the Musgraves were closely linked with the Eden Valley from the earliest times. From what would seem to be relatively small beginnings, the family was in a position to purchase Hartley Castle from Lord Neville of Raby, to whom the castle had been granted after the execution of Sir Andrew de Harcla for failing to resist successfully Robert Bruce's invasion of the north in 1323. From the middle of the fourteenth century Hartley became the seat of the Musgraves and it remained so until the Stapleton Musgrave marriage. Hartley is near Kirkby

Stephen and it is in the beautiful 'Cathedral of the Dale', St Stephen's Church, that several members of the Musgrave family are buried, including Sir Richard, who according to tradition killed the last boar to roam on Wild Boar Fell, a tradition that gained more credence when the chancel and Musgrave Chapel were restored between the years 1847 and 1851, for Sir Richard (who died in 1409) was found to have been buried with his lady and a wild boar's tusk.

The Musgraves certainly did much to improve Hartley Castle, and another Sir Richard was responsible for enlarging the old fortress into a mansion in about 1660. However, it was Edenhall that was to become the family's chief home. At the beginning of the eighteenth century Thomas Pennant made his celebrated Tour to Alston Moor and recorded that, 'Scarcely a wreck is left of the castle which stood on a eminence above the village of Hartley. For a long time it was kept in good repair; and with Edenhall alternately inhabited, but was demolished by the late Sir Christopher Musgrave who removed the material to repair his seat.'

The first member of the family of whom there is record is Peter de Musgrave, who lived in Musgrave village during the reign of King Stephen. Then during the reign of Henry III a Thomas de Musgrave was Sheriff of Westmorland. He was also an executor of Robert de Vipont, or Veteripont, Baron of Appleby, and he also seems to have granted some land in the Orton area to Conishead Priory. The list of the various Musgrave achievements is a long one, until we reach the Sir Thomas who married Joan de Stapleton, daughter of Sir William de Stapleton by whom the Musgraves came by Edenhall. Sir William himself had inherited Edenhall and Alston manors by his marriage to Joan's mother, Margaret de Veteripont, daughter of Nicholas de Veteripont of Alston.

Sir Richard Musgrave, who had been created a Knight of the Bath at the coronation of James I, was advanced to a baronetcy in 1611. The eighth baronet, Sir Philip Musgrave, born in 1794, was educated at Eton and Christ Church College, Oxford, and represented Carlisle in two Parliaments. It was he who entirely rebuilt the family mansion at Edenhall in 1821, dying six years later in 1827. His son, Sir Christopher, built the lodge which is still standing and ordered extensive repairs to the parish church.

However renowned the members of the Musgrave family were, the family is perhaps better known for the legendary 'Luck of Edenhall', a glass goblet described as 'a tall tumbler of old fashion glass, green and specky, expanding in easy curve from the bottom upwards and terminating in a graceful lip, and enamelled with a geometrical design of crimson, blue and yellow'. The 'Luck' was kept in a leather case ornamented with scrolls of vine leaves, and on the top of the monogram IHS, which would point to the vessel's having at one time been some kind of chalice. As Dr Todd, the antiquary, noted: 'From the predatory habits which prevailed on the Borders, it was not safe to have the vessels made of costlier metal', and he goes on to cite the ecclesiastical canon of the reign of King Athelstan "*Sacer calix fusilis sit, non ligneus*" – 'Let the holy chalice be fusile', not of wood, which might imbibe the sacred wine. It seems the Luck of Edenhall was used for imbibing, however, and Philip, Duke of Wharton, an imbiber in his short life if ever there was one, and one who would have enjoyed using a cup once used for sacred purposes, is said to have been the author of 'The Drinking Match of Edenhall.'

God prosper long from being broke
  The Luck of Eden Hall!
A doleful drinking bout I sing,
  There lately did befall.
To chase the spleen with cup and cann
  Duke Philip took his way;
Babes yet unborn shall never see
  The like of such a day.

The 'stout and ever-thirsty duke' continues in ever more doleful drivel till 'many a gallant gentleman lay sick upon the ground'. The poem does not actually suggest that the 'Luck' itself is being used. The 'fairy' origin of the chalice is related in several ballads, and these make very much better reading than Wharton's drinking song. There are several versions of the story based on the theme that elves or fairies were found to be drinking at St

Cuthbert's Well, passing the cup round, when it was snatched away from them either by a page-boy, as in one version, or by a knight returned from the wars, as in another, and they utter the ominous quatrain:

> If that cuppe
> Shall breake or falle,
> Farewell the lucke
> Of Edenhalle.

The ballad which seems to me the best tells how the page of Sir Philip Musgrave seeks to call a doctor for the Lady Isabel and meets a 'weird woman' on the way to Penrith:

> 'O, whither dost run thou little foot-page,
> As swift as hawk on wing?'
> 'For life, for life, to Penrith town
> I run the leech to bring!'

The boy notices that the woman has 'glamour in her eye' and takes in her warning that if the doctor should fail he should seek the fairy's spring. Predictably the latter course becomes necessary, and the boy, after watching the fairies for a while, decides to take the cup 'for the sake of his dear ladye' and finds the fairies' admonition written on a scroll. However, all ends happily:

> Sir Ralph de Musgrave made a feast,
> For joy over his ladye;
> And the little foot-page he stood by her chair,
> And blithest of all was he.
>
> Sir Ralph de Musgrave built a church,
> In sweet St Cuthbert's praise,
> That men might know whence came the lucke,
> And think thereon alwayes.

There is also a painting of the 'Luck of Edenhall', drawn from a photograph of the precious vessel which is kept safely in the Victoria and Albert Museum. Perhaps we should not be surprised that like the fairies Sir Ralph and his Lady Isabel have disappeared, since I have not been able to find their names anywhere in the long list of what Camden called 'the martial and warlike family of the Musgraves'. There is no doubt, however, that the church is dedicated to St Cuthbert.

What may be seen today is largely the rebuilt church of 1834, but there was a church on the same site as early as the reign of King Stephen. In about the year 1298 Edward I granted the church at Edenhall to the Augustinian friars at Carlisle, who from that time supplied a priest until the time of the Dissolution of the Monasteries. For instance, it is recorded that, in 1299, 'John de Ludam, deacon, was presented to this church by the prior and convent of St Mary, Carlisle; who assigned to him for his support the whole altarage of the church, and moiety of the land and meadow of Edenhall and four pounds of silver out of their chamber yearly.' The church is well worth a visit for the many monuments to the Musgrave family it contains, and in the east window there are two early fourteenth-century figures.

Edenhall, which had been united with Langwathby since Bishop Appleby brought the two benefices together in 1380, now forms the United Benefice of Edenhall, Langwatbhy and Culgaith.

Before processing on towards Langwathby, it is worth recalling that in the *Gentleman's Magazine* for the year 1791 there is a reference to a local custom: 'It was customary for the lads and lasses of the neighbourhood to assemble at the Giant's Caves on the third Sunday in May, where they partook of a sweetened drink provided by the lasses, and the day was called Sugar and Water Sunday; they afterwards adjourned to the public-house, where the lads returned the compliment in cakes, ale, punch and other refreshments.' These caves were on the north bank of the River Eamont near Highbarn Cottage. The outing must have been fun in those halcyon days before the Band of Hope rested its dead hand upon it.

The road from Edenhall to Great Salkeld, the B6412, leads directly northwards, running parallel with the Eden, which, in a meandering way, runs due northward for a while also. The river divides Great Salkeld from Little Salkeld, but it is my intention to veer off northwards on the west side of the river to look briefly, alas, at two very important villages, Great Salkeld and Lazonby on the west side, then Kirkoswald, Glassonby and Little Salkeld on the east bank, before returning to Langwathby.

Great Salkeld

The name appears first in the Wetheral Priory Register as 'Salchild', and had I not seen that, I would have thought the '*keld*' part of the name to be the Old Norse for a spring, as in Cold Keld or Kelbarrow – but not here. This is 'the sallow wood' from the Old English '*salh*' and '*hylte*', and as the two Salkelds, Great and Little, are on either side of the River Eden, it seems likely that the sallows grew down to the banks of the stream at one time.

It seems that the Salkelds were once a royal manor, held by Ranulph de Meschines, for the name appears among other Cumberland manors that were escheated when he became Earl of Chester in 1120. What is certain is that the manor of Great Salkeld was granted by Richard I to Alan le Sauser, and this grant was confirmed by King John. It subsequently reverted to the Crown and was granted with Penrith to Alexander, King of the Scots. From that time onward the histories of the two manors have been inseparable, so that after William of Orange ascended the throne and granted many manors to his favourite, Bentinck, whom he created Duke of Portland, Great Salkeld eventually became part of the estate of the Duke of Devonshire.

As it was once held by the kings of Scotland, Salkeld was often called 'Salkeld Regis' in early documents, or 'King's Salkeld' from the tenure of Great Salkeld by the King of Scots by grant of Henry III in 1242.

Great Salkeld parish church is one of the many in the area dedicated to St Cuthbert. It has a broad late fourteenth-century west tower which looks as though it were built as some kind of defence, and has been thus compared with similar structures at Burgh-by-Sands and Newton Arlosh. There is a fireplace on the first floor of the tower. Although much, if not most, of the church is Victorian, there are traces of Norman work, and there is an effigy of a priest, Thomas de Caldebec, dated 1320, presumably at one time the incumbent of the parish, but not as well known as an eighteenth-century vicar of Great Salkeld, William Nicolson.

Bishop Nicolson was born in Plumbland on Whit Sunday 1655, the eldest son of the Reverend Joseph Nicolson, rector of Plumbland, and his wife, Mary, daughter of John Brisco of Crofton in Thursby. His early schooling was at Dovenby in Bridekirk, but he went up to Queen's College, Oxford, in 1670, becoming Bachelor of Arts in 1676 and Master of Arts three years later. In 1788 he was sent abroad to Leipzig to learn German and the languages of northern Europe, at the expense of Sir Joseph Williamson, the Secretary of State. While he was in Leipzig he translated from English into Latin an essay of Robert Hooke towards a proof of the motion of the earth from the sun's parallax, which was printed at the cost of the professor who had suggested it.

Back in England in 1680, he contributed descriptions of Poland, Denmark, Norway, and Iceland to the first volume of Moses Pitt's *English Atlas*, while the second and third volumes contained his accounts of the empire of Germany; he also undertook supervision and completion of the description of Turkey for a later volume. Although gaining a reputation 'of a drinking fellow and boon companion', Nicolson was ordained deacon in December 1679 and became chaplain to Bishop Rainbow of Carlisle, which ensured his speedy preferment in the diocese. In 1681 he was appointed vicar of Torpenhow, but after eight years he resigned the living to his brother-in-law in favour of the vicarage of Addingham. However, Bishop Rainbow had done more than this for him, for he had become senior canon of the cathedral in 1681 and archdeacon the following year. It was in the same year that he was instituted as rector of Great Salkeld, which was annexed to the archdeaconry, and the village became his home, where 'He built outhouses at the rectory, constructed new school buildings, and erected a wall around the churchyard'. Nicolson kept all his preferments until he succeeded Bishop Rainbow in 1702.

Described as 'the most colourful and dominating of personalities', he lacked the deep spirituality of Bishop Rainbow. During his years as archdeacon he had involved himself in senseless quarrels but in most important matters Nicolson was a very good bishop, a fine administrator, and being a native of the area he understood the needs and aspirations of his people in a way little known at the time. In this respect I cannot help thinking of a Westmorland man, Thomas Barlow, who in the seventeenth century was bishop of Lincoln for sixteen years and never once during the time visited his cathedral. Nicolson was bishop of Carlisle for about the same number of years and seems to have spent some two-thirds of his time in the diocese. The accounts of his Visitation tours of the diocese make very good reading. The Bishop gave praise where it is due but was harsh in his criticism where he could see that the clergy were not 'up to scratch'. For instance, he praised Kirkby Thore as being in the 'best repair of anyone in the diocese' but Stapleton had a roof 'so miserably shattered and broken, that it cannot be safe sitting under it'.

Bishop Nicolson was once described as 'a proud, haughty, ignorant, peevish and huffing writer', 'huffing' here meaning bullying and not what it might imply today. But his importance as a local historian is considerable, and we should be grateful for his energy and concern. It was he who arranged the Machell manuscripts into six folio-size volumes, and his own collections relative to the Carlisle Diocese comprise four similar-sized volumes, all of which were invaluable to his relation Joseph Nicolson, who in collaboration with Richard Burn was the author of *The History and Antiquities of Westmorland and Cumberland*, published in 1777.

Bishop Nicolson had married Elizabeth Archer, the daughter of John Archer of Oxenholme, in Westmorland, and there were three sons and five daughters born of the marriage. In 1718 the Bishop was offered the diocese of Londonderry, which carried a salary over three times the size of Carlisle, which was at that time only £775. He accepted on the initial understanding that he could remain living in England, but the King told him this was not possible. On Easter Day 1719 he preached his last sermon in Carlisle Cathedral.

Bishop Nicolson remained in Ireland until the end of his life. In 1727 he became Archbishop of Cashal, but he died only five days after his appointment on 14 February, and was interred in Londonderry Cathedral.

Also associated with Great Salkeld is Lord Ellenborough, who conducted the defence of Warren Hastings before the House of Lords in 1787. Born Edward Law, at the vicarage in Great Salkeld, where his father was vicar in 1750, he was educated at Cambridge and called to the bar when he was thirty. He rose to be Attorney-General and later Chief Justice and, as Lord Ellenborough, died in 1818. Other eminent men born in the parish were George Benson, the Dissenter, and Rowland Wetheral, the mathematician.

Great Salkeld was unusual in having a school from particularly early times. It was founded in 1515, ten years earlier than the famous school at Sedbergh. The schoolhouse was built by subscription in 1686. In 1856, after a lapse of some years when nothing was taught, a new building was erected which was 'an ornament to the village' and has remained so ever since.

Lazonby

Lazonby was written 'Leisingebi' in 1165, which looks as though the name means 'the village of the freedmen'. It is built on a hill and situated about 2½ miles north of Great Salkeld. Here the Eden swings westward after passing Lacy's Caves and continues from then on, apart from a short swing eastward at Armathwaite, in the north-westerly course that will eventually lead it to Carlisle.

Lazonby grew in importance through the railway, which at one time seemed to divide the village in two. The parish originally consisted of the townships of Lazonby and Plumpton Wall, the latter being known in earlier times as Old Penrith, where the Roman camp was situated. The first possessors of the manor were the Stuteville family, from whom it passed through successive heiresses to the Morvilles, the Multons and the Dacres. By the forfeit of all Leonard Dacre's estates, Lazonby became Crown property but it was eventually allowed to Francis, Lord Dacre of the South. In 1716 the manor was sold to the Musgraves of Edenhall.

St Nicholas's Church stands on a small hill on the east side of the village street. It is Victorian, designed by Anthony Salvin in 1863, but built on the site of an earlier church. Sir Hugh de Morville had granted the church at Lazonby to Lanercost Priory, and it is interesting to note that Bishop Nicolson on one of his Visitations recorded that there were many Roman monuments from the fort at Old Penrith converted into gravestone.

Among the eighteenth-century vicars of Lazonby was Dr John Brown, who while in the parish wrote poetry and plays, one of which, *Barbarossa*, was produced by David Garrick in London. Garrick also acted in the drama, which included such lines as:

> Now let us thank the eternal Power; convinced
> That Heaven but tries our virtue by affection,
> That oft the cloud that wraps the present hour
> Serves but to brighten all our future days.

Brown had been born in Northumberland, but when his father became vicar of Wigton he attended the grammar school there and went on to St John's College, Cambridge. He was ordained into the Carlisle diocese and appointed vicar of Morland in 1743, moving to Lazonby nine years later. There he remained until 1757, when he was succeeded by his father, who had retired from Wigton. John Brown became vicar of Newcastle in 1761 but died by his own hand four years later in London, in one of his many fits of depression.

Brown was a friend of Dr Johnson and his circle, his words for an oratoric; *Saul*, are said to have been used by Handel, and his sermons on such subjects as slavery and free compulsory education made considerable impact. Before he died, he had arranged to visit Russia, where the Empress, hearing of his views on education, had offered him £1,000 in expenses to give her advice.

It was Brown who preached the Assize Sermons in the September of 1746 when those who had supported the second Jacobite Rebellion were brought for trial in Carlisle. He spoke of 'the justice of our excellent laws, tempered by the wise mercy of a gracious king'. There was little mercy shown, and six weeks later many of those who supported the Pretender were hanged, drawn and quartered, their heads impaled on the gates of the city.

For many who live in the villages around Lazonby, the name may be most associated with the famous bakery, Bell's of Lazonby, whose vans visit places as far away as ... well, there may be one in our village at the moment!

Plumpton Wall

The second township of Lazonby parish was Plumpton Wall, situated to the west across Lazonby Fell. The two villages are about six miles apart, and Plumpton rests between the A6 and the River Petteril, while the main Lancaster to Carlisle railway line and M6 motorway run parallel with the river. Today Plumpton is a parish in its own right, with its own church, St John's, designed by Sir Robert Lorimer in 1907. Prior to this there was only a chapel-of-ease, also dedicated to the Evangelist, built in 1767 at the expense of the local people. It is almost certain that there was a chapel at Plumpton even before that date, if the pattern that I have noticed in other Cumberland parishes prevailed there.

Plumpton is famous for the Roman station, Voreda, known locally as 'Castlestead', situated about a mile and a quarter from the village. The site has never been properly excavated, but there have been many inscriptions found there dedicated to Jupiter, Mercury, Mars and several other gods and goddesses. The station was occupied from the time of the Emperor Hadrian until the fourth century, and it is known that the second cohort of the Gauls was stationed there during the third century.

The site of the station is easily seen on the west side of the A6 and covers an area of about three acres. In the sixteenth century Edward Threlkeld, who was archdeacon of Carlisle and vicar of Salkeld, spoke of the ruins of an 'old town, a mile compass about'. It seems that there was an external settlement around the Roman station. In 1732 it was described as follows: 'On the west side there is a descent, as usual, towards the river, and great ruins of a town. The ruins of buildings also on the other sides, particularly on the east and south, are very remarkable.' This explains why the people in Elizabethan times thought this must be the site of Old Penrith. Today, as a result of steady farming through the past two centuries, there is nothing to see of these old buildings, and it has only been in the process of draining or roadworks that anything is unearthed. No doubt many of the stones are incorporated in the walls around.

The positioning of a station at this point was to link the road from Keswick via Threlkeld and Greystoke with the main route from Brougham to Carlisle. At Old Penrith the west-east road crossed the greater road and continued on more or less northward towards Brampton and the Roman Wall. Also there was another minor road leading westward towards Old Carlisle, the Roman Olenacum, situated a mile south of Wigton.

Although in general part of Inglewood Forest, Plumpton was a 'hay' – that is, a special hunting ground. The hay of Plumpton, often referred to as Plumpton Park, was enclosed in the time of Henry III and described by Camden as 'very large, and formerly set apart by the Kings of England for the keeping of deer'. Henry VIII 'prudently planted the area with men, being almost a frontier between England and Scotland'.

The park was, it seems, a separate manor and was partly in Lazonby and partly in the neighbouring parish, Hesket, which for obvious reasons is really Hesket-in-the-Forest. Hesket consisted of Upper and Nether Hesket, better known today as High and Low Hesket, Armathwaite, Calthwaite, Itonfield, Petteril Crooks and Plumpton Street. As these places look more naturally towards Carlisle than Penrith, they are beyond the scope of this book. Perhaps one day I shall write about them, but I must now return to Lazonby and take the road northwards, only for a mile or so, and cross over the Eden to arrive at Kirkoswald.

Kirkoswald

Kirkoswald, as the name suggests, means simply 'Oswald's church' and is named after the famous king of Northumbria who was killed in battle by the pagan King Penda of Mercia. I suspect that many people know that much about St Oswald but that the other facts of his life are less well known. However, a saint who has some sixty or so churches dedicated to him in England and to whom chapels or altars are dedicated in Prague and Ratisbon deserves to be better known.

Oswald was the son of Ethelfrith, King of Northumbria. When the kingdom was seized by Edwin in the year 616, he fled into Scotland and eventually reached Iona, where he was converted to Christianity. When Edwin died in 633, Oswald returned to his kingdom, where the tyrant British king Cadwalla, who had assumed power, was defeated and killed at a battle which took place near Hexham at Hevenfelt. It is said that Oswald set up a wooden cross and before the battle invited his soldiers to join him in prayer. After the victory, which was seen as an answer to prayer, he set about the task of converting his people and invited missionaries from Iona to come into Northumbria. The first bishop sent was a total failure, but when he was replaced by St Aidan the mission met with success. Oswald gave Aidan the island of Lindisfarne as his episcopal seat, and the saint established a monastery on the island, close to Oswald's own stronghold at Bamburgh.

Through the number of conversions it was possible for Oswald to bring unity to the two parts of Northumbria which had been hostile to each other for so long, Bernicia and Deira. He had married Cyneburga, a Wessex princess, and stood as godfather to his father-in-law, Cynegils, King of Wessex. Oswald died in 642, during the battle of Maserfield, in Shropshire, fighting against Penda. He was only thirty-eight years old.

As one approaches Kirkoswald from the Lazonby direction, one may just see the church to the right, though it is completely hidden from the village itself by a large hill which seems to divide the church from the village – but there are very good reasons for this. The church is situated by the ancient holy well, St Oswald's Well, and in fact a small stream flows right underneath the church, as we shall see, so it is understandable that the village should develop around the bridge over Raven Beck and extend up the hill for much more important than the church in medieval times was Kirkoswald Castle, situated only a short distance to the south-east. In 1670 Sandford wrote: 'This great castle of Kirkoswald was one of the fairest fabrics that eyes ever looked upon. The hall I have seen is one hundred yards long.'

The castle has been built in about the year 1200 by Ranulph d'Engayne, Lord of Cumberland, who granted the manors of

Lazonby and Kirkoswald to Robert de Trivers. Lord Ranulph's great-grand-daughter Ada Engayne married Simon de Morville, and their son Sir Hugh gained permission to crenellate the castle and to enclose a deer park. (Incidentally, it is important not to confuse this Hugh de Morville with his namesake who was one of St Thomas à Becket's murderers and owned property in Westmorland, in particular Pendragon Castle.) Kirkoswald passed from Sir Hugh to his two daughters, Ada and Johanna, since his wife, Helewisa de Stutteville, had no sons, and through the two girls to their respective husbands, Richard de Lacy of Egrement, who died very soon, and Richard Gernon.

In 1314 the castle was burnt down and destroyed by the Scots, but in about 1320 it was rebuilt by the de Multon family. Some 150 years later the castle was described as 'newly built', and in the early years of Henry VIII's reign the great hall and chapel were built by Thomas, Lord Dacre. He also 'encompassed the castle with a large ditch for better security and beautified it at great expense'. In 1561 Lord Dacre is mentioned as living in the castle, and in 1580 the house or castle was 'one of the chief mansion houses' belonging to the heirs of the late Leonard Dacre. In 1604 Lord William Howard proceeded to dismantle the building, and on 28 June 1610 a grant was made to Sir William Anstruther 'of all the materials of the decayed castle of Kirkoswald, also lease of the lands on which the castle stood and the gardens'. it was in 1620 that materials from Kirkoswald were transported to Naworth, and from that time onward there are several references to materials being sold. In 1622 Sir John Lowther bought timbers for his roof at Lowther Hall; in 1633 Sir Timothy Fetherstonhaugh paid Lord William Howard £3 for some stone, and before this time the roof of the chapel had been taken to Naworth.

In 1675 Edmund Sandford wrote: 'This great castle of Kirkoswald was once the fairest fabricks that ever eyes looked upon. In this Grand Castle, I was some sixty years ago when there were many Towers, Chambers and Chapels.' It seems Sandford was exaggerating, for it is unlikely there was ever more than one chapel, and he described the hall as a hundred yards long, when he presumably meant feet. Nevertheless, the castle was once a very impressive building, and in 1688 Thomas Denton noticed it as 'a bare shell or heap of stones'.

The fate of the castle, however, has not been shared by the College, which is still the home of the Fetherstonhaugh family. The college at Kirkoswald was nothing like as important as the one at Greystoke, neither was it to be so long-lived. It was founded late in 1523 by Thomas de Dacre and his wife, and we may see here where the idea came from, for Dacre's wife was Isabel de Greystoke. The college may have been founded because of 'the low state of religion in the place', but it only lasted long enough to see two provosts, John Herring and Rowland Threlkeld, the latter being at the time also rector of Dufton, vicar of Lazonby, vicar of Melmerby, rector of Halton, in Lancashire, and prebendary of Carlisle. Did he have much time for the college? It seems he did. It was well administered and when the Dissolution came in 1547 it was a flourishing establishment that the King's Commissioners took over. Though the provost resisted their intention of making him 'an example for the terror of others', he was forced to hand over an inventory of the college's goods. For a while he remained staunchly in office but capitulated in 1548. Anyone interested in this remarkable man should consult *Our Cumberland Village* by Colonel T. Fetherstonhaugh, which is a particularly good account of the history and traditions of Kirkoswald.

Built on a hill, Kirkoswald is one of the most attractive villages in what may be termed the Penrith area. The college is at the bottom of the hill on the south side of Raven Beck which runs through the village, and almost directly opposite its gates is the small wrought-iron with an over lantern leading down 'Church Flags' towards the churchyard where St Oswald's Well is situated: this is outside at the west end of the church. There is no bell tower here but there is one on the hill behind the church, built in 1897 to replace 'a charming wooden structure' of 1747. Some of St Oswald's is late twelfth and early thirteenth century, while more is fourteenth and fifteenth. A distinctive feature is the way the chancel is so much higher than the nave, approached by four steps rather than the usual one or two found in most churches. There are many memorials to the Fetherstonhaugh family who have lived at the college since Henry Fetherstonhaugh of Southwaite purchased the property in 1590.

Although developed from an early pele tower, the front of the college was entirely built in 1696; as Nikolaus Pevsner says, it could be anywhere in the Home Counties and is 'progressive for Cumberland'. The gateway, however, is early Victorian. Of the past occupants of the house, Sir Timothy Fetherstonhaugh is best known for his supporting Charles II in at the battle of Worcester in 1651, an 'offence' for which he was beheaded by the Cromwellian government.

The village street leads uphill, past the small cobbled square on the west side with the reminder, 'Enough that valour fills the space between', the Fetherston Arms Hotel on the east side, beyond that a garden with quite the largest onions growing I had ever seen, and the Methodist chapel dated 1871 with the brightest door-knob. All was well impressed on my mind as I set off towards Nunnery Walks, feeling sad at the thought of another Timothy Fetherstonhaugh, remembered in the church, who survived only a few hours after the injury he received from the fall of a tree in front of the college on the 5th day of April 1856. He had been aged forty-five.

The faithful page he mounts his steed,
And soon has crossed green Irthing's mead,
Dashed o'er Kirkoswald's verdant plain,
And Eden barred his course in vain.

Addingham

Addingham is three miles south of Kirkoswald, on the east bank of the Eden. The name is one of the oldest Anglian names in Cumberland, and it is strange that it is the name not of a village but of an ecclesiastical parish which includes the villages of Glassonby, Little Salkeld, Hunsonby, Winskill and, much further to the east, Gamblesby. 'Addingham' is 'the village of Adda's people', and such a form is quite common east of the Pennines. It is not known who Adda was, but his name lives on locally, for St Michael's Church is situated at Addingham, although to the uninitiated it seems to be in the village of Glassonby.

The reason for this is that the original village, where an earlier St Michael's Church stood, was washed away when the Eden flooded and changed its course at some unknown date. In 1794 Hutchinson noted that, 'Only part of the churchyard remained, the buildings having been washed away by the river.' This earlier village was situated about a mile west of Glassonby, right on the banks of the river, and is thought to have been destroyed some time between the middle of the fourteenth century and the close of the sixteenth. The date 1350, given in the short guide for sale in the present church as the year of the church's destruction, is, I suggest, mistaken, although that year many villages lost as much as a quarter of their populations through the plague.

The present church is well worth a visit and was largely restored to good advantage as recently as 1983. In 1704 Bishop Nicolson noted that the church was in very poor order and had no monuments. This is certainly not so today. An unusually long drought in the summer of 1913 made it possible to rescue several items from the river-bed: a Norman grave-slab, the base of a cross and a hogback coffin. All these may be seen, together with two large pieces of a ninth-century cross and in the churchyard a large wheel-head cross, the Addingham Cross, brought from the river some hundred years earlier.

Downhill from the turning to the church is the small village of Glassonby. In the courtyard of Glassonby Lodge is a well mount that once stood at Lowther Castle, but there is little else of historical interest here. I do not mean to suggest that Glassonby is ugly, for the opposite is true: the village is built on the side of a steep hill where a small beck runs down to meet the larger Hazelrigg Beck, beside which is a cairn circle of small upright stones, some fifty feet in diameter. Although I mentioned another, larger stone circle in the opening chapter, the thought of such things brings me conveniently to Little Salkeld, since Long Meg and her Daughters stand south of Glassonby near that small village where there was once a chapel-of-ease of Addingham parish. Today Little Salkeld is best known for its watermill on Sunnygill Beck. This is one of the few watermills in working order which is used for its original purpose, to grind corn into flour – or, as we have to say now to make the matter clear, to 'stone-grind' corn into flour, which was for centuries the traditional way. There is a tea-room at the mill, and it is open to the public in the afternoons of Monday, Wednesday, Thursday and Sunday from Easter until the end of October.

Little Salkeld village is situated on a small hill which looks down towards the Eden and, although they are obscured by trees, towards Lacy's Caves, named after Lieutenant-Colonel Samuel Lacy, the owner of Salkeld Hall in the eighteenth century. The caves are natural but much enlarged, and this would not have been all that difficult since the sandstone is very soft. It has been suggested that the Colonel employed a man to pose as a hermit in order to impress the 'antiquity' of the caves on his guests. The caves have been advertised in one of the *Walking East of Eden* pamphlets and seem destined to grow larger and larger.

Salkeld Hall itself has a late eighteenth-century look about it and is situated south of the village. Only the front of the house is eighteenth century, and the earlier building was the home during the Civil War of George Salkeld, who, because of his Royalist sympathies, was forced to part with the hall for a 'trifling sum' to Colonel Chomley, who made large additions to it. Colonel Lacy bought the house in 1790 and after making many alterations sold it to Robert Hodgson.

Hunsonby and Winskill

Hunsonby, 'the dog-keeper's village or hamlet', and Winskill, 'the windy shieling or shepherd's summer-hut', are situated east of Little Salkeld, some three miles south of Glassonby. Together the two hamlets formed a single township in Addingham parish. In 1881 they had a population of 280 between them, their children attending the school that had been founded for the benefit of the township by Joseph Hutchinson, a yeoman of Hunsonby, in 1726. This was a Free School and was 'open to all the children of the township indefinitely, free of expense'. Such schools were not uncommon in the smallest of places, and there was a similar school at Maughanby, a mile south of Glassonby, of an even earlier date, 1634, founded by Edward Mayplett, vicar of Addingham from 1591 until 1636. Needless to say, both schools have long since been closed.

Situated higher up the Sunnygill Beck than Little Salkeld, Hunsonby also used to make use of the water: in 1937 an open-air swimming pool was built in the village to commemorate the coronation of King George VI and Queen Elizabeth. This is still a feature of Hunsonby, although the water now comes from the mains. Perhaps I should add that at Hunsonby Sunnygill Beck is understandably known as Hunsonby Beck!

Taking a circuitous route through Kirkoswald and returning through the villages on the east side of the Eden has meant that we left the Penrith to Alston road before entering Langwathby, and we crossed the river without the experience of the large girder bridge which was cast across after the stone bridge was washed away in the floods of 1968. The present structure has ever since then been described as 'temporary', but it does the job well and would be unlikely to be dislodged by flood, so that it seems destined to remain there for the foreseeable future.

Langwathby

As its name suggests, Langwathby is the main crossing of the River Eden of the Alston road. It is 'the village by the long ford'. The 'lang' part could also mean wide, and the 'wath' is clearly the Old Norse '*vaþ*', meaning a ford.

Records show that Langwathby's history has been closely linked with that of Penrith. Henry I held the manor as a royal desmesne, a situation that continued during the reign of King John, and Henry III granted it to Alexander, King of Scotland, in 1237. It later reverted to the English Crown after the defection of John Baliol, and Richard II granted it to Ralph Neville, so that it eventually became the possession of Richard, Duke of Gloucester, after the death of the Kingmaker. Langwathby then remained Crown property until William III granted the manor to Hans Willem Bentinck, first Earl of Portland, who sold it in 1787 to the Duke of Devonshire.

Langwathby is first mentioned in a record of 1159, where it appears as 'Langwadebi'. The form 'Langanby' by which the village is still known to a large number of local people did not appear until 1576.

As I indicated earlier, the railway was to make quite a difference to the development of the place, though Langwathby never ceased to be a village built round a fairly large green. Today the Shepherd's Inn remains, but in 1847 there was also the Coach and Horses, the New Inn and the Highland Laddie, while in 1897 there was a Fish Inn too, run by Tyson Weir who was also a farmer. In 1897 there were three carpenters, a dressmaker, a shoemaker, a blacksmith, a butcher and one or two other shops besides. William Cheesbrough was the miller at Langwathby mill, John Wilson a carrier and coal merchant, and George Dalton the postmaster, all going to make up a thriving community, whereas today the village is more of a dormitory for Penrith.

St Peter's Church at Langwathby was built in 1718, but it is almost certainly standing on the site of a chantry of the thirteenth century which was dedicated to the Blessed Virgin Mary and mentioned in the *Valor Ecclesiasticus* in Henry VIII's reign. It is thought to have been Bishop Appleby who united Langwathby with Edenhall in 1380, a situation that prevails today, although Culgaith was added to form a united benefice in 1980.

The main road, the A686, continues towards Melmerby and Alston beyond, but it is necessary to glance some three miles eastward and take notice of Ousby, which some will know for its camping and caravan site. There is more of interest than that!

Ousby

The majority of early records suggest that this was 'Ulfr's by', 'the village or hamlet belonging to Ulfr', but the forms are varied and fascinating. In 1268 there is 'Ulvesby'; in the register of Wetheral Priory 'Ulsusby' appears in 1306, while a link with Ullswater, 'Ulfr's lake', is seen in an Assize Roll of 1279, where 'Ullesby' is seen. Nothing resembling the modern spelling is to be found until the sixteenth century.

The village is situated on the west side of Sunnygill Beck, named after the Norwegian St Sunniva, and appears in the Wetheral Register as 'Sunnivegile' in 1237.

Unlike most of the manors in the area, Ousby was divided up at an early date. During the reign of Henry III Julian Falcard and William Armstrong each held a moeity, and soon after Henry le Sergeant and Patrick de Ulnesby each held an eighth part. (Notice another strange spelling of the place-name in 'Ulnesby'.) What remained was divided between Carlisle Priory, Lanercost and the prior of St John of Jerusalem, and much was sold and distributed among the families of Crackenthorpe, Salkeld, Crofton, Beauchamp and Raughton. It seems the Crackenthorpe family by 'purchase, or otherwise' retained the manorial rights.

The parish church dedicated to St Luke is situated a little outside the village to the east, but although there has been a church on the site since the thirteenth century, what one sees today is the restoration carried out in 1858. There is one treasure in Ousby church, an effigy carved in oak of a cross-legged knight dressed in mail armour, wearing spurs and resting his feet on a little dog. There are only two such figures in the country, the other at Pamber, in Hampshire. This crusader is well worth seeing.

From Ousby a straight line might be drawn on the map due north through Melmerby and on to Gamblesby. What is interesting about these villages is that they each take their name from an early owner. Melmerby, which lies about half way between Penrith and Alston, is 'Melmor's village'. Melmor also appears in Gospatric's charter in the eleventh century as a landowner in Allerdale. His name is Gaelic and post-Christian, since it means 'the servant of Mary'.

Melmerby, one of the most attractive villages on the East Fellside, is bounded on the east by Hartside Fell and on the other sides by the parishes of Addingham and Ousby. Today, linked with Ousby and Skirwith, it forms a united benefice, but in early days the parish, though small – only two miles in length by one in breadth – was always important, having its own market and an annual fair. It was in 1335 that Sir Robert Parving was granted the right by Edward III to hold a weekly market on a Wednesday and hold a fair at the festival of St Peter ad Vincula – that is, on 1 August. This was a ratification of the original grant by Edward I to John de Wigton.

The manor was all part of Adam fitz Swein's barony and was first held by the Wigton family in the reign of Henry III. Margaret, the sole daughter and heiress of John de Wigton, married firstly Sir John Gernon and secondly Sir John Western. By neither of these noble husbands did she have any children, so that she granted Melmerby to Sir Robert Parving, who was the King's Serjeant-at-Law and afterwards became successively Lord Chief Justice of the King's Bench, Lord Chancellor and Lord High Treasurer. Sir Robert was succeeded by his sister's son, who took the name of Parving; he died in 1380 and was succeeded by the Threlkelds. It was a co-heiress of the Threlkeld family who married Thomas Pattenson, and so brought the manor into the possession of the family that held it at the beginning of the nineteenth century.

There are still members of the Threlkeld family living in and around Melmerby. The place has an interesting history. Some time between 1307 and 1327 John de Denum is recorded as keeping a garrison of twelve men at his tower of Melmerby, which was 'always well defended by the grace of God against the Scots to the great damage and loss of their men'. This early tower was, in about 1570, developed into a dwelling house. In 1610 it was recorded that, 'Melmerby is the name of the town parish and capital messuage there, now the dwelling house and seat of the Threlkelds', and in 1675 that: 'A little from Kirkoswald you have Mel Melmerby: an ancient square hall house of the name of Threlkeld; younger branch of Sir Lancelot Threlkeld of Threlkeld.'

Today Melmerby Hall shows traces of many stages of building. One wing is early seventeenth century, but the main block of three storeys is eighteenth century. All is hidden in trees, as is the little parish church next to it.

When the fashion of establishing collegiate churches began in Cumberland and resulted in the founding of the college at Greystoke, it was owing to Sir Robert Parving, who besides gaining a grant for a market had hoped to establish a college at Melmerby. The college was to have eight priests, and the first master, Richard de Caldecote, was appointed in 1342. Had not Sir Robert died a year later, before the college really began, there is little doubt that it would have flourished as did Greystoke and, later, Kirkoswald, for its foundation was to have been on a sound footing: 'One message and an oxgang of land in Melmerby together the advowsons of the rectories of Melmerby and Skelton were assigned for the support of the college.' It was laid down that the Bishop of Carlisle could not remove any member of the college 'except for reasonable cause', and the founder reserved to himself and his heirs the right of patronage. It was arranged that: 'The master and his chaplains should repair daily in the morning at dawn to the church at Melmerby, vested in surplice, amice, and black cope, and sing the Canonical Hours devoutly and distinctly, matins and prime according to use of Sarum; which done, immediately without pause, the mass of the Blessed Virgin should be celebrated by one of the chaplains.' After the first Mass, two other chaplains were to offer Masses at the altar of St Nicholas, one Mass of St Nicholas himself and the other of St Margaret.

The present church at Melmerby is dedicated to St John the Baptist and, although standing on the site of the earlier thirteenth-century building, is mostly the Victorian reconstruction of 1895. Some years earlier, in 1849, the church had been repaired and reseated, the latter necessarily, it seems, for in 1703 Bishop Nicholson noted that, 'The seats appropriated to the men are backed and good; but those for the women are low and mean'. The men and women sat in separate parts of the church, as was customary in many parishes.

When the Bishop visited, the arms of the Threlkeld family were in the east window; now they may be seen on a stone set in the sanctuary floor. However, the most distinctive feature of Melmerby church is the embattled tower at the west end. It was built in 1848 with a higher turret on which stands the weather-cock, but some restoration work was undertaken in 1928.

The way from the church brings one into the main part of the village, past another strange turreted building, once a school, and leads almost inevitably, for visitors at any rate, to the village bakery, which is housed in a converted barn overlooking the thirteen-acre village green. Here the hundred per cent wholewheat flour stone-ground at Little Salkeld watermill meets its destiny. On the upper floor of the bakery is an excellent display of the history of bread, with particular reference to Cumbrian tradition. All the baking at Melmerby is done in a wood-fired brick oven and is of a very high standard. Not all in the village is bread and cakes: there is ale to be found at the Shepherd's Inn.

Gamblesby

The Alston road begins to climb dramatically once Melmerby is passed, but although one has steep fellside on one's right at the beginning of the ascent, on the left one continues to look down towards the Eden Valley and the little villages that nestle up, as it were, to the rising slope. The first of these is Gamblesby, situated about two miles north of Melmerby and linked to it by an attractive minor road which takes one past the farm called 'Todhills', 'the fox hills'. Gamblesby is the kind of Cumbrian village I enjoy most, where farms and farmyards are an integral part of the centre. When in 1868 the architect C.J. Ferguson was employed to design the little church of St John's, the site chosen was a small tarn which was presumably part of the farmyard next door, where today there are several peacocks strutting about with the hens. The tarn was filled in and the church rests on a foundation of concrete; the building, with a nave and chancel in one in the thirteenth-century style, is of local stone carted by volunteers from a nearby quarry. Here is one of the few churches with an apse in the area covered in this book.

Gamblesby has always been part of Addingham parish, as we have seen, and in early days it was linked with Glassonby to form one seigniory. In 1201 the manors are recorded in a writ as having been given by Henry I to Hildred of Carlisle and Odard his son. Here also the names of Gamel and Glasson appear as earlier holders of the land, and there is a reference to 'Gamelesbi' as early as 1177.

North of Gambleby is another hamlet of Addingham, Unthank situated on Hazelrigg Beck, and two miles or so further on Renwick, which is beside the Raven Beck and indeed gives it the name. Renwick is really 'Ravenswick', where '*wic*' is the Old

English for a village or, often, a diary farm. It is thought in this instance that the name of the beck is a back-formation from the place-name.

Renwick was originally held by the Stavely family, but later it appears among the estates forfeited by Sir Andrew de Harcla. Edward III granted the manor to Robert Eglesfield in return for the manor of Hide, in Laleham, Middlesex, and in 1341 Eglesfield settled it upon his newly founded college at Oxford. The college proved to be a careful landowner and in the reign of Charles II issued an order to the tenants at Renwick 'to scour and cleanse the watercourse to the lord's mill from the bottom up to the mill with wall and thatch, and bring the millstones to the same, and grind their corn thereat, paying a 24th multure'. (A multure was the toll paid to the miller which was enforceable.) The people were further forbidden to cut down trees for timber, 'except what shall be set out to them by the steward for the necessary repairs of the houses'. The college also worked a colliery on Renwick Fell, and the subject of mines and mining leads our thoughts naturally towards Alston, which is approached from Renwick by the road through Haresceugh, 'the hare's wood', which brings us back to the A689.

Alston

The road climbs steadily upwards between Alston Moor and Gilderdale Forest, bearing due eastward until Leadgate and then veering northward to Alston, the highest market town in England, situated a thousand feet above sea-level.

Alston was known as 'Aldenby' in the twelfth century, but early in the thirteenth, about 1208, the first reference to 'Aldenstoun' appeared. The place takes its name from an early owner, Halfdan; owing to Norman-French influence, the H was dropped, though a reference to 'Haldeston' is made in an assize roll of 1279.

In 1164, or a little after, William, King of Scots, granted Alston to William de Vipont, and in 1208 Ivo, de Vipont's son, was granted a second charter. This was very valuable land for beneath its soil lay veins of lead from which a certain amount of silver could be extracted. As the metal could be designated silver, it automatically belonged to the Crown, and the Norman kings were quick to exploit the situation. The royal miners were a privileged community and were under special protection. In 1235, for instance, Henry III offered his miners 'the liberties and free customs to which they had been accustomed in the time of his predecessors'. Two years later it was declared 'that any one who disturbed the miners should forfeit £10 to the king'.

There were many disputes over this rich region, the King of Scots claiming that the manor of Alston lay within his domain which he held by homage. So much was true, but the manor was a different matter from the minerals that lay beneath the soil! The mines at Alston were placed under the protection of the sheriff of Carlisle by Henry I, and from this time there are mentions of 'the mine of Carlisle' and references to various uses of the lead. '555 cartloads of lead delivered to the sheriff of Northumberland to be carried to Caen' at a cost of £24.15s. Again, in 1179, £66.13s.4d. was paid for '100 cartloads of lead delivered to brother Simon to work at the church at Clarevill' – it is particularly satisfying to think that Alston lead went towards building the famous Cistercian abbey at Clairvaux founded by St Bernard, and in 1181 more lead was needed there and supplied.

The first time the mines were referred to as 'the Alston Mines' was in 1224; at about that time the bailiff was ordered 'to allow Cumberland miners to have free passage through all his master's land, forest as well as other lands, to buy Victuals'. Something of the conditions in which the miners lived and worked is seen in these early records. For instance, we find that they often lived together in sheilings, and in such a situation would appoint one of their members as Coroner and another as Bailiff or King's Sergeant. All problems arising out of this communal living were decided and judgements put into effect by these two. However, there were times when miners were dispersed working in pairs, so 'that they should no longer exercise the above privileges'. For their 'liberties and immunities' the miners were obliged to pay 10 marks a year to the King's Exchequer at Carlisle.

In 1359 an outside speculator seems to have gained possession of the mines for a while, for we find that, 'Tilman of Cologne shewing that he has taken the mines of silver, copper and lead in

Aldeston More from the freemen of Aldeston More at farm for certain payments to the king and them for the same, and had hired and will hire labourers for the mines, the king has taken him and the labourers while working in the mines into his special protection.' It seems the mines did not often bring in profit, which is probably why Tilman of Cologne held on to them for such a short time. Something of the problem is seen in a record of 1414, the year before Agincourt:

> William de Stapleton and his tenants at will in this manor and their predecessors from time beyond all memory had annually paid at the King's Exchequer at Carlisle ten marks for the mines at Aldenston which in the exchequer run by the name of the mine of Carlisle, though for fifty years and more before that time the mine itself had ceased and been profitless to them to their great and manifest injury; the king therefore granted them the aforesaid mines, with all the commodities, profits, emoluments, liberties, and franchise and immunities, whatsoever thereunto belonging to be holden for ever by the annual payment of the said ancient sum of ten marks.

From such beginnings did the original mining industry in the area rise and fall, so that there are few records until the region was opened up again at a later date. It was in 1690 that what became known as the Rampgill Vein at Nent Head was discovered to be very rich, and then in 1704 the London Lead Company was formed, often known as the Quaker Company. It was to become the chief employer in the area for over two centuries, but the owner of the land was, perhaps surprisingly, Greenwich Hospital. After the first Jacobite Rebellion in 1715, all the estates of the Earl of Derwentwater became forfeit to the Crown, and eventually, in 1753, all the Derwentwater interest in Alston Moor was granted to Commissioners of the Greenwich Hospital for Seamen. At the beginning the Commissioners held on to one mine and leased out the rest, some thirty mines in all, but in 1736 the London Lead Company was granted a long term lease on the more profitable mines.

The history of the Pennine mines is thoroughly documented in two important books: *A History of Lead Mining in the Pennines*, by Raisbrick and Jennings, and *The Lead Miners of the*

Northern Pennines in the Eighteenth and Nineteenth Centuries, by C.J. Hunt. Both are in print.

Alston with its cobbled street is built on a hill and situated where the River Nent meets the South Tyne. From a distance the spire of St Augustine's Church gives the place a look of importance which is not undeserved. Although the town is in Cumbria and on the Tyne, ecclesiastically the parish is in the Newcastle diocese. The first record of a church in the town is during the reign of Henry II, who appointed Galfrid as rector. Was he the first? There is no way of telling, but it would seem unlikely.

St Augustine's – and this is Augustine of Canterbury and not the great fourth-century bishop of North Africa – was built in 1869 when the earlier church, of 1770, was completely demolished. Even the 1770 church was, of course, a replacement of the medieval building which was in the rural deanery of Corbridge and in Durham diocese. There are several records of the canons of Hexham claiming their right to appoint a priest at Alston, but it seems that the king had a prior claim and there are two instances of Edward I presenting priests to the parish. However, soon the king does hand the advowson – that is, the right to appoint a priest – over to the priory and their 'successors for ever'. During the reign of Henry III Alston was worth 40 marks a year, which is four times the value of the mines!

Inside the church designed by J.W. Walton is the Derwentwater clock which came from Dilston Hall and was presented to the people of Alston by Greenwich Hospital in 1767. The clock has only one hand and is of the sixteenth century. The bell by which it chimes was cast in 1714 and recast in 1845, but in 1978 the clock was restored and set up in the church 'as a working exhibit'.

It was at the Cross in Alston market-place that John Wesley addressed a group of 'quiet staring people, who seemed to be little concerned one way or the other'. This was better than the reception that he was to receive four years later at Clifton, near Penrith, when, as he said, he preached to 'a civil people, who looked just as if I had been talking Greek'. Wesley had ridden over the moor to Nenthead and moved on to Alston to preach there at midday. This unpromising beginning did nothing, however, to hinder the growth of Methodism in the town, and since 1797 there has always been a thriving chapel in Alston.

There is still much in Alston to attract the eye, but sadly one of its strangest features died when mining ceased in the 1950s. This was the five-mile-long underground canal known as 'the Nent Force Level'. It was part of the mine drainage begun in about 1770 and designed by John Smeaton, the engineer famous for building the Eddystone Lighthouse, although the man who had perhaps more to do with the Level's construction was Richard Walton. Nevertheless, the Nent Force Level was often referred to locally as 'Smeaton's Folly'. It was a remarkable feat of engineering and in the early years of the nineteenth century became a popular tourist attraction. One young enthusiast described his experience as follows:

> I can remember the entrance of the Level, when the walk to the waterfall was one of the most picturesque in the district ... The waterway was 9ft by 9ft with about 5ft of water. The air was fresh and still, and your voice echoed strangely if you shouted. For long distances it is quiet, but there are places near the upper end where falling water makes a great noise.
>
> The Level varies a good deal in width and height. In some places it is necessary to be flat in the boat and shining a light you could see the top. The boats are propelled by stakes driven into the right hand side of the wall.
>
> We had often heard older people talk of the adventures and lovely nights they had spent in Nent Force Level dancing in Jennie's Dancing Loft. The Dancing Loft is near the south end of the canal section of the waterway. It is a platform cut out of solid rock, just above water height. The floor is smooth rock, a lovely dancing floor, and parties of young people used to go up the Level in boats, with good supplies of candles, taking their music with them. It must have been exciting and very romantic to hear the music and voices echo and see the lights twinkling on the water.

Today all signs of the Level have disappeared, but Alston is justly proud of the South Tynedale Railway Preservation Society's magnificent work in re-opening part of the old railway line as a tourist attraction, so although it may be said that the underground days of Alston have passed, all is active on top!

It is now time to retrace our steps and return westward towards Penrith. As the Eden Valley comes once again into sight, with the great Lakeland hills beyond, we might just discern the much smaller hill of Penrith Beacon tufted with trees but with the roof of the Beacon Tower rising above them. It is at the beacon that this portrait of Penrith and the East Fellside will end.

Penrith Beacon

Of 5 October 1429 a commission was issued to Richard Neville, Lord Warden of the March, and other notable leaders including Hugh Lowther and Christopher Curwen, 'to array all men-at-arms and other fencible men, whether hobelers or archers dwelling in Cumberland'. (A 'hobeler' was a light horseman and had nothing to do with lameness.) The commission continued to instruct the leaders to lead their men to the coast 'or other places as occasion required'. Of particular interest was the command that 'Bekyns' were to be set up in suitable places to give warning of the arrival of the enemy.

The beacon system had been developed in the time of Henry III, and in 1403 it had been made statutory. It was employed on both sides of the Border, and by 1455 the Scots had a complete system in operation by Act of Parliament where the strength and brightness of the fire signalled different messages. One 'baile is warning of their cumming', and so on.

Penrith Beacon appears in a list of beacons issued for the year 1468. It was to communicate with the one at Dale Raughton, which was situated on the high ground above the farmhouses of Old Parks, Kirkoswald, an altitude of 660 feet. For its own part, Penrith could receive news from the beacon on the high tower of Carlisle Castle and send it south to the beacon on Orton Scar.

The fire on the castle tower at Carlisle was the usual practice, for the wardens were commanded that, 'Every man that hath a castle or tower of stone wall, upon every fray raysed in the night, give warning to the countrie by fire in the topps of the castle or tower in such sort as he shall be directed from his warning castle, upon paine of 3s.4d.'

Beacons were usually situated on hills between six and seven hundred feet which were fairly close to habitation and easily reached by horse and cart to carry the straw or hay for the fire. Penrith Beacon was a little higher, at 937 feet, and the 'Pike' is well worth visiting with its eighteenth-century red sandstone tower built in 1719 and restored in 1780. The tower is square-shaped with a pyramid roof and round-arched windows, and it stands up against the skyline on its tree-bowed hill. The trees are relatively recent, but we catch a glimpse of what the scene looked like before their arrival. In 1794 Anne Radcliffe, the author of *The Mysteries of Udolpho* and other Gothick novels, noted: 'The town consisting chiefly of old houses, straggles along two sides of the high north road, and is built upon the side of a mountain, that towers to great height above it, in steep and healthy knolls, unshaded by a single tree.' At the time there would have been none of the copious building between Drovers Land and Meeting House Lane and Beacon Edge, no Wordsworth Street, no Graham Street or Macadam Way, nor the complex of little streets where most of the Penrith people now live. Anne Radcliffe was looking down on what is now the town centre. 'Penrith, despite its many symptoms of antiquity, is not deficient in neatness,' she noted with typical eighteen-century emphasis on 'neatness'. 'The houses are chiefly white, with door and window cases of the red stone found in the neighbourhood. Some of the smaller have their doors dates of the latter part of the sixteenth century.' The town lies, Mrs Radcliffe concludes, 'spreading prettily along the skirts of the mountain, with its many roofs of blue slate, among which the church rises near a dark grove'.

Up on the Beacon a five-year-old boy went riding with a friend some time in 1775. Somehow he became separated from his partner, his 'encourager and guide', and found himself quite alone. Feeling that he was lost, he dismounted and led his fell pony downhill until he came to a dip in the hillside. It was there that he saw an old decaying gibbet-post and, although the murderer's body had gone, strange initials set in the turf; sensing the horror of the place, the boy hurried away into the wind and was relieved to see a girl carrying a pitcher of water on her head close to the small tarn near the summit. The Beacon was not always to hold horrors for Wordsworth, for on another occasion, he was able to speak of:

The Border Beacon, and the waste
Of naked pools, and common crags that lay
Exposed on the bare fell, was scattered love,
A spirit of pleasure and youth's golden gleam.

Index